JONI MITCHELL'S *BLUE*

Oxford KEYNOTES

Series Editor   KEVIN BARTIG

Sergei Prokofiev's Alexander Nevsky
KEVIN BARTIG

Arvo Pärt's Tabula Rasa
KEVIN C. KARNES

Aaron Copland's Appalachian Spring
ANNERET FAUSER

Rodgers and Hammerstein's Carousel
TIM CARTER

Arlen and Harburg's Over the Rainbow
WALTER FRISCH

Beethoven's Symphony No. 9
ALEXANDER REHDING

Claude Debussy's Clair de Lune
GERMINDER KAUR BHOGAL

Brian Eno's Ambient 1: Music for Airports
JOHN T. LYSAKER

Alfred Schnittke's Concerto Grosso no. 1
PETER J. SCHMELZ

George Bizet's Carmen
NELLY FURMAN

Jean Sibelius's Violin Concerto
TINA K. RAMNARINE

Puccini's La Bohème
ALEXANDRA WILSON

Antonín Dvořák's New World Symphony
DOUGLAS W. SHADLE

Beethoven's String Quartet in C-sharp Minor, Op. 131
NANCY NOVEMBER

Gioachino Rossini's The Barber of Seville
HILARY PORISS

Laurie Anderson's Big Science
S. ALEXANDER REED

Shostakovich's Symphony No. 5
MARINA FROLOVA-WALKER & JONATHAN WALKER

Manuel de Falla's El amor brujo
CAROL A. HESS

Berlioz's Requiem
JENNIFER WALKER

Dolly Parton's Jolene
LYDIA HAMESSLEY

Shostakovich's Lady Macbeth of the Mtsensk District
PAULINE FAIRCLOUGH

Joni Mitchell's Blue
LLOYD WHITESELL

Oxford KEYNOTES

JONI MITCHELL'S *BLUE*

LLOYD WHITESELL

Oxford University Press is a department of the University of Oxford.
It furthers the University's objective of excellence in research, scholarship,
and education by publishing worldwide. Oxford is a registered trade mark of
Oxford University Press in the UK and in certain other countries.

Published in the United States of America by Oxford University Press
198 Madison Avenue, New York, NY 10016, United States of America.

© Oxford University Press 2026

All rights reserved. No part of this publication may be reproduced, stored in a retrieval system, transmitted, used for text and data mining, or used for training artificial intelligence, in any form or by any means, without the prior permission in writing of Oxford University Press, or as expressly permitted by law, by license or under terms agreed with the appropriate reprographics rights organization. Inquiries concerning reproduction outside the scope of the above should be sent to the Rights Department, Oxford University Press, at the address above.

You must not circulate this work in any other form
and you must impose this same condition on any acquirer.

CIP data is on file at the Library of Congress

ISBN 9780197686836 (pbk.)
ISBN 9780197686829 (hbk.)

DOI: 10.1093/9780197686867.001.0001

The manufacturer's authorized representative in the EU for product safety is
Oxford University Press España S.A. of Parque Empresarial San Fernando de Henares,
Avenida de Castilla, 2 – 28830 Madrid (www.oup.es/en or product.safety@oup.com).
OUP España S.A. also acts as importer into Spain of products made by the manufacturer.

Series Editor's
INTRODUCTION

OXFORD KEYNOTES REIMAGINES THE canons of Western music for the twenty-first century. With each of its volumes dedicated to a single composition or an album, the series provides an informed, critical, and provocative companion to music as artwork and experience. Books in the series explore how works of music have engaged listeners, performers, artists, and others through history and in the present. They illuminate the roles of musicians and musics in shaping Western cultures and societies, and they seek to spark discussion of ongoing transitions in contemporary musical landscapes. Each approaches its key work in a unique way, tailored to the distinct opportunities that the work presents. Targeted at performers, curious listeners, and advanced undergraduates, volumes in the series are written by expert and engaging voices in their fields, and will therefore be of significant interest to scholars and critics as well.

In selecting titles for the series, Oxford Keynotes balances two ways of defining the canons of Western music: as lists of works that critics and scholars deem to have articulated key moments in the history of the art, and as lists of works that comprise the bulk of what consumers listen to, purchase, and perform today. Often, the two lists intersect, but the overlap is imperfect. While not neglecting the first, Oxford Keynotes gives considerable weight to the second. It confronts the musicological canon with the living repertoire of performance and recording in classical, popular, jazz, and other idioms. And it seeks to expand that living repertoire through the latest musicological research.

Kevin Bartig
Michigan State University

CONTENTS

ACKNOWLEDGMENTS *xi*

1 Canons, Attachments, Epiphanies *1*
2 Outpouring *15*
3 Zeitgeist *35*
4 Artistry *55*
5 Epilogue: Only a Phase *79*

NOTES *89*

BIBLIOGRAPHY *101*

ADDITIONAL SOURCES FOR READING AND LISTENING *107*

INDEX *111*

ACKNOWLEDGMENTS

THANKS GO TO KARL Ferris and Norman Seeff for permission to reproduce their photographs. Thanks to fellow Joni fans Les Irvin, Rachel Avery, Rachel Hottle, Nicole Biamonte, Nancy Murphy, Peter Kaminsky, Megan Lyons, and Udayan Sen for help, conversations, and support. This book is my love letter to Joni.

FIGURE 1.1 Joni Mitchell receiving the 1995 Billboard Century Award (AP).

CHAPTER 1
CANONS, ATTACHMENTS, EPIPHANIES

At the turn of the present century, the pop music critics of the *New York Times* convened "to select 25 albums representing turning points and pinnacles in 20th-century popular music." Among the chosen few was Joni Mitchell's fourth studio album, *Blue*. Here is their time-capsule citation:

> JONI MITCHELL: *Blue* (Reprise, 1971). A restless woman travels, falls in love and longs for what she left behind as she moves on; in the background 1960's ideals crumble. Joni Mitchell turned unsparing autobiography into sparse songs that quietly rejected symmetry and happy endings while they poured out her yearning. As she ushered in a confessional mode for pop songwriting, few of her emulators noticed that her seemingly unguarded revelations were so finely constructed.[1]

In compact, restrained prose, they celebrate Mitchell's music for its fervent emotion, exquisite craftsmanship, and vivid reflection of a definite place and time. I plan to explore each of these topics at a more relaxed pace in the chapters that follow. For now, I want to draw attention to the point the critics are making about Mitchell's significance for music history—namely, that she changed its course. This is one way to value her achievement as a songwriter.

Other distinguished media outlets have followed suit by granting official honors to *Blue*. In 2006, *Time* magazine placed the album on its list of "All-TIME 100 Albums" ("the 100 greatest and most influential musical compilations since 1954").[2] In 2020, *Rolling Stone* promoted *Blue* to #3 on its list of the "500 Greatest Albums of All Time" (moving up from #30 when the list first appeared in 2003).[3] And *Blue* holds the top position among the "150 Greatest Albums Made by Women," published by *NPR* in 2017.[4] Lists like these are controversial in that they enshrine subjective preferences as definitive judgments and perform a kind of cultural gatekeeping by conferring prestige on a finite set of artists admitted to the ranks of the great. For a conflicting view, we might compare the list published by *Pitchfork* in 2004, where *Blue* barely makes the cut, even within a generous latitude of acclaim per decade, ranking #86 of the "100 Best Albums of the 1970s."[5]

But what do the "greatest" list-makers mean when they call an album great? What criteria are they using, among the many to choose from: artistic quality? originality? profundity of expression? influence? enduring significance? universal appeal? Stripped of any clues as to how it is measured, the title of greatness is an empty endorsement. It has the effect of creating a canon of works to be admired and emulated beyond the time of their creation—a repertoire of "classics," to echo *Rolling Stone*. Musicologist Jim Samson observes that a canon "tends to promote the autonomy character, rather than the commodity character, of musical works."[6] That is, canonization emphasizes the timeless qualities of a musical recording, lifting it out of the living but unstable environment of changing fashions, competing scenes, and the market economy. It also obscures the complex history of ideological flashpoints by which some musicians have been legitimated or privileged over others, so as to "reinforce the identities and values of those who exercise cultural power."[7] (Canons have long been used to privilege composers of "classical" music over those of "popular" music, men over women, and so on.) Members of social or creative groups who find themselves on the wrong side of an entrenched value hierarchy or who struggle to gain access to the channels of music distribution are justified in their suspicion of taste-making institutions and official canon formation. The writers of the *New York Times* "Mileposts" piece are more transparent than other canonizers in making one criterion of value explicit right from the start: their aim is to recognize "turning points" in the history of popular music. By crediting Joni Mitchell with ushering in a new, confessional mode of expression, they acknowledge the songwriter's extraordinary influence and status as a true innovator.

Honor rolls shine a light on musical creators, what they were up to and what they accomplished. What happens when we shift focus to the listener? Literary critic Rita Felski makes a fundamental distinction between two scales of aesthetic value: cultural prestige and personal attachment, or how we as individuals "are drawn to certain works because they matter to us."[8] The two scales of value interact with each other, but at root they are disjunct, following different logics and reflecting different types of experience. "Our consciously held beliefs about . . . cultural value do not line up perfectly with our attachments (those works that captivate and change us)."[9] When critic Ann Powers commemorated *Blue* on the album's fiftieth anniversary, she adduced further reasons for its glowing reputation: "It became a classic—the most beloved Joni album, the most written about, the one that encapsulates the essence of her talent."[10] Here is another way to value Mitchell's music, not for its artistic achievement but for its ability to inspire devotion.

In 2021, the Los Angeles-based pop group Trousdale released the single "Always, Joni," a Gen Z fangirl tribute in the form of a love letter. The lyrics weave together references to twelve of Mitchell's classic songs, with four allusions to *Blue* packed into a mere two lines: "cuz *all I really want* is *a case of you* / with a *little green California* view." The vocals are swoony and lush, but the words are bittersweet. The band members express their relationship to the revered artist in personal terms by casting her in the role of an ex-lover they're still stuck on: "Why you gotta break my heart all over again?" They adopt a genre Joni is known for—the torch song—to capture what she means to them as an emblem of passion and vulnerability, pouring out their adoration in the key of heartbreak.

For personal testimony about the impact of *Blue* when it was new, we can turn to an account by Irish novelist Colm Tóibín, from an anthology in which noted writers pay homage to the record albums that played a defining role in their lives. Tóibín was sixteen, "a confused boy in a small town," when *Blue* was released in 1971.[11] Intrigued by a notice in the *Irish Times,* he bought the only copy at the local record store and for the next three weeks became obsessed, listening to it "first thing in the morning, last thing at night, and all day in between."[12] Too naive to grasp some of the references to drinking and drugs, he had no trouble understanding the feelings expressed.

> When it came to the next track, "River," I was again sure I knew what she felt. There was a river in our town as well, and a main road out of the town. I had got out a few times and liked the look of things in the city. Joni Mitchell's music, her voice so filled with the smoke of experience and vulnerability and need, was a way to have for myself a world elsewhere, planning my life in that world quietly, keeping the dullness of things at bay.[13]

Something about Mitchell's self-expression on *Blue* encouraged the formation of strong personal bonds between a performer and a listener. Not only did young Colm love her songs, he identified with them: "I lived with those songs as though they were about me just as much as they were about the woman who wrote them and sang them."[14] And even though the life experiences of the twenty-seven-year-old artist had no parallel in the life of the teenage boy, her music held powerful meaning for him. Somehow it spoke to his own circumstances and channeled his own unformed desires. It gave him a glimpse of a life to be lived.

I loved the experiences described in these songs, full of lost love, willful wanderings, moments of bliss and hope against bitter regret for pure romantic experiences which had taken place in deep intimacy. I loved the sheer glamour of the wanderings and longings described and then the piercing pain that came with them. I wanted to live like that and instead I was going back to boarding school.[15]

In his youthful attachment to *Blue,* Tóibín opened himself up to its intermingled bliss and pain. As a gay person on the cusp of adulthood, he heard something in its emotional tenor that resonated with his awareness of "being not quite right."[16] In fact, looking back, he wonders if he was playing the LP the wrong way around, side 2 first, "so that for me it ended with the song 'Blue.'"[17] In contrast, when Ruth Charnock listened to the same album some thirty years later, she always skipped the title track. "'Blue' dragged and held on too tight. 'Blue' was fragile, wavering. 'Blue' sounded exhausted and felt exhausting to listen to—so deflating after 'Carey's' flirty flights; such a cold-water shock."[18] For young Ruth in 2003, the tracks that epitomized the special allure of the album were "All I Want, "Carey," and "California": the flirty ones, the ones that "keep desire in endless, joyful play," the ones suggesting that "the 1960s free-love project has been genuinely liberating for women."[19] Among the promises she heard in *Blue* at the age of 21:

- You can have a life with your own creativity at its center.
- You can have joyful encounters with men and leave without regret.

- You can vocalize your desires and no one will shut them down.
- Life can be a series of absorbing scenes that you move through.
- You do not have to grow out of your attachments to these promises.[20]

In her optimistic, euphoric reception of Mitchell's emotionally turbulent music, Charnock was reconstituting the album and listening through a filter, extracting "scenes of untrammeled freedom and potential" and disregarding the reverberations of bitterness and regret.[21]

When we approach *Blue* from the perspective of actual listeners, it sheds its monumental quality and becomes a pliant collection of songs to be disassembled and reframed. Rather than adhering to an official story, it generates an evolving field of personal significance, meaning "many different things to different people."[22] One person's idea of what *Blue* represents may differ markedly from someone else's based on their selective relationship with the music. This speaks to the way listeners actively co-create the soundtracks of their lives, but it also speaks to the generosity of Joni's musical persona and the richness of her gifts. In the first song on the album, when she exclaims "I want to write you a love letter," some of us take it personally; we want to write a letter to Joni in return. When she sings "I want to make you feel free," we know the first-person character is speaking to her lover, but on another level, it sounds like the *artist* is saying to *us*: Here are the songs of my heart. Feel free to treasure them as you will, to comb through them for the joy, tenderness, or heartache you need to hear.

So a composite field of meaning is generated when various listeners interact with Joni's art, each bringing their own social background and individual concerns to the encounter. Listeners form attachments based on what they find meaningful in the music, whether that be self-empowerment, emotional wisdom, or ideas about a life well lived. But the listening experience is not defined by meaning alone. An engagement with art involves something more visceral, an appeal to the senses that can bypass rational thought in its intensity. "Encountering a new painting, viewers may intone critical pieties gleaned from the Sunday supplements to impress their friends," Rita Felski observes. "But they may also burst into tears for reasons they cannot explain."[23] We can see this very thing occurring in an online video posted in 2021 by Daniel Profeta at Dicon Dissectional Reactions, a media channel featuring first-time listening reactions. Daniel introduces himself, thanks his viewers for requesting the title track from *Blue*, and explains, "Here we react to music and I try to figure out what the music and the lyrics mean to me personally."[24] But his usual procedure is derailed by a visceral response to the sensuous aspects of the song. After only one word, Daniel looks stricken and quietly exclaims, "Oh my god." After about a minute and twenty seconds, he suddenly pauses the playback and expresses bewilderment: "What the hell is happening. I'm like crying and I don't even. . . .It's super weird. Holy cow. What the hell is happening right now?" After apologizing for interrupting the musical experience, he tries again, picking up where he left off.

Before a line of text is uttered, before the first-time listener can even begin to assess what the song means, he is struck like a thunderbolt by how it *sounds*: the piano's bleak harmonies, Joni's weary, keening voice. At such a moment, the question is not "what is she saying?" but "how does she do that?" How has she managed to pierce my defenses without warning and overwhelm me with emotion? Why is this music so devastating? Some art critics have spoken of this aspect of the aesthetic experience in terms of *presence*. Hans Ulrich Gumbrecht, for one, distinguishes between meaning and presence in the encounter with a work of art. In his view, all artworks have both a signifying dimension that is understood (or "redeemed," like a token) through an act of interpretation, and a phenomenal dimension appreciated for its material qualities and sensory impact—the elegance of a pattern or curve, the sonic properties of a poem, or the shock of a violent disruption. One's experience of art is "characterized by an oscillation between presence effects and meaning effects."[25] The two aesthetic dimensions exist in productive tension; they need not work to the same end. Music can have a vivid acoustic presence apart from, and supplemental to, any meanings we might ascribe to it. It follows that we can value composers for their ability to deliver that artistic dimension that remains beyond our understanding, that we experience as visceral or awesome or sublime—the power to "fill up our consciousness, crowding out awareness of other things, such that the rest of the world dissolves into nothingness."[26]

Novelist Zadie Smith considers this dimension of music in an essay describing her dramatic conversion to Joni Mitchell fandom. Having grown up without exposure to the artist (in a mixed-race household where they "did not tend to listen to white women singing very often"), during her twenties she found Joni's style of singing incomprehensible and annoying: "a strange, strangulated falsetto—a kind of Kafkaesque 'piping.'"[27] Despite pressure from friends, she remained unmoved and uninterested in getting to know the music better. All the more surprising, then, when she suddenly falls for Joni at the age of 33. Driving to a wedding in Wales with her husband, her mood sour, craving a sausage roll, she becomes aware of an irritating noise coming from the car speakers—Joni's song "River." She begs her husband to switch it off, against his objections ("It's *Joni Mitchell*. What is *wrong* with you? Listen to it—it's beautiful!").[28] But then they stop to visit the ruins of Tintern Abbey in its peaceful valley, and the setting works a kind of magic. "I wandered inside, which is outside, which is inside. I stood at the east window, feet on the green grass, eyes to the green hills, not contained by a non-building that has lost all its carved defenses. Reduced to a Gothic skeleton, the abbey is penetrated by beauty from above and below."[29] Focused on that immersive and porous beauty, while her husband quotes Wordsworth, she finds herself humming an unaccustomed tune, and something breaches the walls in her mind. "I hated Joni Mitchell—and then I loved her. Her voice did nothing for me—until the day it undid me completely."[30] From that day, listening to Mitchell's music brings on uncontrollable tears.

It is this instantaneous and unconscious reversal that Smith puzzles over. Who *was* that previous version of herself? How is it possible to pivot from hating something to loving it so unreasonably? Her answers hinge on the notion of attunement, that is, being open to the right wavelength. For Smith, the unbidden shift from negative to positive listening felt like a lowering of defenses and a retuning of her aesthetic sensibility. "Now . . . I feel this deep current running between us. I think it must have always been there. All Joni and I needed was a little attunement."[31] The underlying image of the listener as an adjustable instrument is evocative, given Mitchell's experiments with retuning the guitar. But this matter aside, what I find most striking about Smith's testimony is the basis of her newfound connection to the music: she completely overlooks meaning in favor of presence. "I should confess . . . that when I'm thinking of Joni Mitchell it's *Blue* I'm thinking of, really . . . . And it's not even really the content of the music that interests me here. It's the transformation of the listening."[32] No mention of love troubles or living on your own terms. When Smith spells out why she thinks *Blue* is a "great album," it's all about the intensity of the aesthetic experience: "An emotional overcoming, disconcertingly distant from happiness, more like joy—if joy is the recognition of an almost intolerable beauty."[33] She values the artist for the immediacy and impact of her musical ideas, her "miraculous" key changes, her ability to turn the listening experience into "something soaring and positive and sublime."[34]

Gumbrecht would file all such perceptions under the heading of "epiphany," a term he adopts to sketch out a fuller account of presence effects. Aesthetic experience offers certain moments of intensity that we cannot find in our everyday environment. Such intense feelings are ephemeral—we have no hope of holding on to them—and unforeseeable: "We never know whether or when such an epiphany will occur . . . . If it occurs, we do not know what form it will take and how intense it will be: there are no two bolts of lightning . . . that have the same form and no two orchestra performances that will interpret the same score in exactly the same way."[35] Art has the potential to transport us to an existential state (whether we call it "clarity" or "rapture") grounded in a bodily response that seems to provide a momentary release from meaning. An epiphany is a glimpse of a different mode (whether we call it "preconscious" or "preconceptual") that feels closer to just being.[36] Gumbrecht suggests that we long for presence effects precisely because our everyday environment is so dominated by consciousness. "Rather than having to think, always and endlessly . . . we sometimes seem to connect with a layer in our existence that simply wants the things of the world close to our skin."[37] If those things are beautiful or charming or deeply moving, so much the better. In an epiphany, we enjoy the work of art for what it *is*, rather than for what it represents. For critic Michelle Mercer, listening to *Blue* is a "religious experience," causing her to feel chords as colors, animating new reaches within her, luring her to another time and place.[38] Zadie Smith would agree, "Those songs, those exquisite songs! When I listen to them, I know I am in the debt of beauty."[39]

Over the years, Joni Mitchell's album *Blue* has been singled out as a new departure in songwriting, a treasure chest of personal insight, and a pinnacle of musical artistry. What is it about the music that makes it worthy of such claims? We will have a chance to ponder this question in the following chapters, each from a different angle.

FIGURE 2.1 Joni Mitchell with guitar case, 1969 (Library and Archives Canada 3598197).

CHAPTER 2
OUTPOURING

IN LATE 1967 JONI Mitchell moved from New York to Los Angeles, where with David Crosby's support, she was able to make her debut record while enjoying an unusual degree of creative control. Word quickly spread about the new arrival and the quality of her songwriting. Mitchell's first West Coast club date was at the Troubadour in West Hollywood, where the shows were well attended and the crowd receptive. *Billboard* reported, "Miss Mitchell achieved rapport with her audience. They sat attentively as she spun stories based on human experiences and personalities which have inspired her writing."[1] Chris Darrow, a regular performer at the venue, adds, "People got quiet for her. She didn't have to ask for it. It came as a result of the presence that she had. She was obviously going to do something."[2] By this time, the Troubadour had gained the reputation as a proving ground for a new brand of artists who would come to be known as singer-songwriters. The venue played an important role in the careers of Carole King, James Taylor, Jackson Browne, and Elton John, among others.

Singer-songwriters were solo acoustic artists who performed original material and cultivated softer musical styles. "While the singer-songwriter becomes highly visible in 1970, in retrospect we can see that the movement emerged in 1968, when Leonard Cohen, Joni Mitchell, and Laura Nyro released important early examples."[3] The ground had already been laid in the mid-1960s for a special focus on personal, poetic expression, as perceived in contributions from musicians including Gordon Lightfoot, Rod McKuen, Tim Buckley, Buffy Sainte-Marie, and Donovan.[4] But there was nothing resembling a stable genre concept until the end of the decade. This new conception of the composer-performer came with a set of values in which authenticity was key. Artists associated with the movement expressed authenticity through intimate performance, a songwriting style recognizably their own, a turn to personal concerns (in contrast to the public concerns which had defined the folk revival), and an impression of immediacy, a "direct line of communication between the artist and audience."[5] These core values are well articulated in a feature on James Taylor from his early years of fame:

> James is being hailed by critics and audiences as the best of the charismatic musician-performers such as Joni Mitchell, Neil Young, and Elton John. Critics call them the new

troubadours—composers who sing their own sweetly simple, but musically adroit songs.

James . . . is very different from the overamplified hard rock singers who dominated popular music in the late sixties. He sounds like a kid sitting by himself on his bed singing his lonely interior monologues. Says one rock writer, "James writes and sings lyrics that you can hear and dig. People want to hear one musician singing his own songs—so they can feel his original emotion more directly and honestly."[6]

Immediacy was fostered by a candid, vulnerable attitude in performance as well as by modes of sound production with minimal dependence on technology. But a strong impression of intimacy and immediacy could be communicated even at a technological remove. In an interview from 1996, when Mitchell mentions the intimate quality of *Blue*, the interviewer responds, "I'd say not just *Blue* but the two albums on either side of it . . . . There was something not just in the songwriting but also in the vocal delivery that made a lot of people feel like you were singing *just to them*. They're sitting home in their room listening to your records and they feel a very intimate connection to you, like you're singing only to them."[7]

Already by the time of her first album, Joni Mitchell was at the forefront of the "new troubadours" with their personal, intimate aesthetic. Three albums later, *Blue* struck many reviewers as a step forward in her development as an artist. In the songs on *Blue* she does more than convey emotions; she "lays her soul bare," she displays a "vulnerability that one seldom encounters even in the most arty reaches of the music business."[8] Some critics doubted whether this exaggeratedly introspective focus would catch on with listeners. Alan Lewis of *Melody Maker* found it hard to relate to her personal narratives as a member of the rock elite, "able to fly on a whim from Laurel Canyon to Amsterdam or Spain or the Aegean Islands." He recognized that "her songs continue to reflect her own reality, but where once the truths she distilled were universal, the songs here tend to be inward-looking."[9] Billy Walker of *Sounds* worried about her authenticity: "Joni Mitchell wears her heart on her sleeve and doesn't care who knows it and this fact alone has alienated her to many who feel that such emotions, because of their apparent openness, must be false."[10] Don Heckman of the *New York Times* ventured a prediction (and how wrong he was): "I suspect this will be the most disliked of Miss Mitchell's recordings, despite the fact that it attempts more and makes greater demands on her talent than any of the others."[11]

In *Blue*, Mitchell explored a confessional mode of musical expression to a greater degree than she had before. Some music historians, such as David Shumway, for instance, see the confessional stance as a defining characteristic of the singer-songwriter movement from the beginning, but contemporary listeners made a distinction between the two.[12] It makes more sense to view confessional expression as *one* of the modes available to singer-songwriters, representing a special heightening of the prized qualities of candor and vulnerability, and emerging as an aesthetic approach only after the singer-songwriter movement was already established. As I define it, confessional songwriting is characterized by:

- *Lyric voice.* A first-person speaker who represents the voice of the songwriter, expressing their thoughts.[13] Though singer-songwriters also tell stories about other people, their use of the lyric voice "encourages personal identification with the artist as subject."[14]
- *Autobiographical detail.* To clothe their own experiences in poetic form, singer-songwriters may choose to retain conventional figures of speech and dramatic archetypes inherited from the ballad tradition. When they speak conversationally instead, including particularities of time, place, and character, they sharpen the perception of vicarious access to their personal lives. Music critic Al Rudis notes such a change in Joni's approach: "Her songs have always been deeply personal, but until now they've been veiled in metaphor and generalized.... On *Blue* she takes a cue from Lennon and gets down to specifics."[15]
- *Disclosure of private thoughts.* The confessional mode takes the introspection of the singer-songwriter to another level by mimicking a stream of consciousness or divulging matters that people would normally shield from public exposure: character flaws, errors in judgment, embarrassing behavior, and psychological turmoil. Joni recalled in 1985: "I remember when *Blue* was first recorded that was the first really confession kind of writing. It was like, nothing left to lose let's spit it out, and when it was finished I went over to a friend's house and Kris Kristofferson was there. I played it. He said, 'Joni, save something for yourself.'"[16]
- *Extreme vulnerability.* In their search for an ever more intense authenticity, songwriters explore extremities of emotion to the point where they risk losing control

in performance. Warmth becomes pathos; sensitivity becomes rawness and fragility. In Meghan Daum's words, *Blue* is "one of the great examples... of emotional bloodletting channeled into the cause of great art."[17]

Some examples from Mitchell's early songs will help to distinguish the confessional mode from the general singer-songwriter aesthetic. "I Had a King," from her first album (*Song to a Seagull*, 1968), uses a lyric voice to divulge private matters—the emotional fallout from a failing marriage. But the governing conceit of the poem places the modern urban couple behind a scrim of romanticized medieval imagery (the king in the castle, the queen in the grove). Language is poetically elevated (*he sings them of wars and wine*), and vocal delivery is formal and controlled except for occasional moments of increased emotional pressure. This song is a perfect illustration of Al Rudis's point: Mitchell has taken material from her own experience (her marriage to Chuck Mitchell), veiled it in metaphor and generalized the situation by way of well-worn tropes from chivalric literature. Folksinger Malka Marom was overwhelmed the first time she heard Joni perform this song in a Toronto coffeehouse: "I was going through a divorce then. And I just felt, I don't know what it was about that song. Talk about a new way of conveying an existential reality. I just started to sob. She sang it so real, so true, as if she was singing for me, she was my voice. She was everybody's voice, she was like a universal voice."[18] For Marom, "I Had a King" opened a direct line of musical communication, conveying personal realities in terms that took on universal relevance. But the song's diction is too conventional, and its manner too controlled to be labeled confessional. Its effect turns on the tension between noble, archaic rhetoric and private anguish.

In the song "Blue Boy" from *Ladies of the Canyon* (1970)—the album preceding *Blue*—Mitchell takes a different approach. Narrative rather than lyric, the song tells of an unnamed "lady" whose lover is coldhearted and condescending. Poetic diction evokes a premodern world of idols, statues, and pilgrims. But neither the third-person perspective nor the metaphorical structure prevents the speaker from conveying the focal character's deep pain and self-abasement. Mitchell's performance has the power to slay the listener with its intensity. She allows her voice to ebb and swell dramatically, to swoon over the simplest words, to waver in the high register and grovel in the low, to crack and fray. "Blue Boy" discloses private thoughts with intense vulnerability, but without the other two qualities (first person, autobiography) that would establish the confessional mode. There is no way to tell whether the story is based on something from Mitchell's own life or on "human experiences and personalities which have inspired her," and the effect is just as powerful either way.

However, the same album does include three songs ("Conversation," "Willy," and "Rainy Night House") which combine the elements of lyric voice, autobiographical detail, private disclosure, and vulnerability to suggest enhanced access to the singer's personal life. The first-person speaker in "Rainy Night House" depicts a romantic encounter with vivid circumstantial detail (*we took a taxi*; *she left you with your father's gun*), fragments of pillow talk, and existential self-scrutiny. She invites the listener to picture her in vulnerable situations: sleeping on a small white bed, under a watchful eye, later abandoned when her lover embarks on a vision quest. Mitchell's delivery is more subtle and less anguished than in "Blue Boy," but she still adopts a mercurial vocal persona, with quick changes of tone, tension, and thickness, to portray spontaneous thought and the flash of urgent feelings. Overall, the first three albums display a wide range of resources available to the songwriter: storytelling as well as internal reflection, artificial as well as colloquial diction, and archetypal romance as well as contemporary social observation. The confessional mode is simply one possible configuration among many, not yet a favored subgenre.

The singer-songwriters of the 1960s didn't invent this mode of expression; it has important roots in the melodramatic suffering of traditional ballads, the personal woes of the blues, and the hard-knock testimonials of country music. It was an aspect of the musical inheritance they were exploring and remaking in their own image. In her wildly original album *Eli and the Thirteenth Confession* (1968), Laura Nyro adapts blues discourse into a confessional voice in the song "Woman's Blues" (*My lover's mouth / Been so good to me / It promised joy for a jailhouse / And a broken key*). She channels the surrealist optics of Beat poetry in "Poverty Train" (*You can see the walls roar / See your brains on the floor*), merging it with blues cosmology (*I just saw the Devil / And he's smilin' at me / I heard my bones cry / 'Devil why's it got to be'*). Many of Nyro's songs resemble a stream of consciousness, but their cryptic lyrics never fully reveal her subjective experience, which remains strangely othered, as we see in the title song from *New York*

Tendaberry (1969) (*New York Tendaberry / Blue berry / A rush on rum / Of brush and drum / And the past is a blue note / Inside me*). Even so, her hyper-expressive performing style reaches out to the listener with its charisma and sensuous appeal. Prolonged passages of hushed intensity, dynamic leaps across a wide vocal range, a willingness to push her voice past the bounds of the beautiful into wails and aggressive harangues—all were important influences on Joni Mitchell's musical style from 1969 to 1972.[19]

Shumway suggests that James Taylor's song "Fire and Rain" (*Sweet Baby James*, 1970) was the first pop song in the confessional mode to become a hit.[20] This song alludes to some very traumatic personal experiences—the suicide of a friend, struggles with drug addiction, the failure of Taylor's band, the Flying Machine to get off the ground—yet the allusions are never explicit. Listeners could only speculate about the obscure private references until Taylor provided an explanation in interviews. His performance is also quite restrained, maintaining the same level of melancholy introspection throughout. To be sure, he takes a subjective approach, embodying an intimate, vulnerable persona relative to prevailing modes of rock manhood. Though it represents a step on the way to confessional songwriting, "Fire and Rain" doesn't quite count as such, by the standards of heightened candor and vulnerability that would soon come into focus.

A better early example would be "Early Morning Rain" by Gordon Lightfoot (*Lightfoot!* 1966), whose cold, drunk, broke, despondent speaker depicts his situation in precisely observed detail. Or Paul Simon's song "America" (Simon and Garfunkel, *Bookends*, 1968), inspired by an actual road trip and resembling pages from a journal (*So we bought a pack of cigarettes and Mrs. Wagner pies; I'm empty and aching and I don't know why*). Or Stephen Stills's song "4 + 20" (Crosby, Stills, Nash, and Young, *Déjà vu*, 1970), in which the speaker makes note of his age and his parents' struggle to escape poverty, then pours out his own troubles: isolation, self-sabotage, inner torment, thoughts of suicide. Vocal delivery is understated, in a musical style recalling blues and country. Stills was 24 when the song was written, so the opening reference encourages an autobiographical reading, in keeping with the aesthetic of "the artist as subject." But whether the experiences are fictional or Stills's own, they give substance to a confessional persona. These examples show individual songwriters, each on their own path, exploring different manifestations of the autobiographical voice, gauging the balance between frankness and discretion, and tentatively lowering their defenses. Out of this creative activity a new poetic configuration is emerging.

In retrospect, it's clear that *Blue* was a turning point, as the *New York Times* critics recognized in the citation that opens this book. As David Shumway puts it, *Blue* "cemented the confessional stance."[21] In the words of Todd Warnke, "*Blue* became the catechism of the singer-songwriter confessional."[22] And according to Daniel Levitin, "*Blue* is the archetypal 'confessional singer/songwriter' album . . . that set the standard for dozens of artists who wanted to pour out their most private feelings to a mass audience."[23] Whereas Mitchell's previous albums feature mixtures of lyric and storytelling trying on various forms of address, *Blue* is single-minded in its lyric perspective: all but one of its ten songs speak in first person. (The exception, "Little Green," is unique in several respects, as we will see.) The opening song, "All I Want," immediately highlights the strong desires pulling the singer this way and that, sending her on a personal search. The travel episodes and emotional peaks and valleys that make up the album seem to unfold from this impulsive source. Gone are the folk echoes and refined diction of her earlier period, replaced by the cadences of ordinary conversation (*Maybe it's been too long / Since I was scramblin' in the street*; *Look out the left, the captain said / The lights down there, that's where we'll land*).[24] Precisely observed details trace Joni's footsteps and align our viewpoint with hers (*The wind is in from Africa / Last night I couldn't sleep*; *Sitting in a park in Paris, France / Reading the news*; *On the back of a cartoon coaster / In the blue TV screen light / I drew a map of Canada*).[25]

The breathless exuberance of "All I Want" releases a stream of sensations, veering at top speed from hate to love and from kissing to lashing out. Life's pleasures and pains hit home with exaggerated intensity; even ordinary activities (dancing, shampooing, knitting) trigger steep highs and lows. This ingenuous persona is not afraid to appear naive or idealistic. She doesn't edit out her petty behavior or jealous feelings but spills the good and the bad with the same gusto. Mitchell's vocal delivery is astonishing in the subtlety of its shadings and the richness of its characterization. Not one line goes by without multiple variations in timbre and strength. She begins in a relaxed, pure head voice (*I am on a lonely road*), then moves into chest voice with sudden tension and urgency (*traveling, traveling, traveling*). One moment (*I hate you some*) she is strident and peevish, the very next moment (*I love you some*) silken and restrained. Her plunge from the thin and breathy "sweet romance" to the round, meaty "baby" with a suggestive bend in pitch is incredibly sexy. At the end of the second verse (*we both get so blue*), the word "blue" sounds tattered and torn, losing tone and pulsating with the motion of her strums over the dulcimer. For "I want to have fun," she lapses briefly into a childlike voice with no vibrato. At the close of the song, she hits the penultimate line (*Want to make you feel free*) with a piercing, unbeautiful quality that adds a dash of bitters to her passionate longing. All in all, Mitchell handles her vocal resources with the skill of an accomplished actor.

The volatile sensibility and interpretive nuance displayed in this song extend over the whole album. Taking a bird's-eye view of its ups and downs, the first song rushes to embrace life with mixed feelings. "My Old Man" beams with happiness. "Little Green" carries dark undercurrents of pain and loss. "Carey" is a joyous release, the most upbeat song on the album. From that peak, we tumble into a trough, the abject depression of "Blue." Side 2 of the LP opens with "California," bright and sunny but longing for home. After "This Flight Tonight," energetic and impassioned, "River" is disconsolate with grief and self-recrimination. "A Case of You" is a postmortem for a relationship that still sings in the blood like wine, "so bitter and so sweet." Finally, "The Last Time I Saw Richard" is one more descent into gloom. But where the high spirits of the opening song were checked by twinges of pain, the pessimism of the closing song is leavened with hope (*Only a dark cocoon before I get my gorgeous wings*).

Most of the songs are new, written in the year since the release of *Ladies of the Canyon* (1970), but "Little Green" dates from 1967, before Joni's debut as a recording artist. Its text exhibits the intricate rhyme schemes and somewhat precious diction of that earlier period; thus it stands out in the context for its heightened artifice. "Little Green" relates events of deep personal significance, while holding them at arm's length by telling them in the second person. Instead of directly admitting "I'm sad and I'm sorry," the subject of the poem reflects, "You're sad and you're sorry, but you're not ashamed," as if observing her own actions and thoughts from the outside.[26] Without any additional knowledge about Mitchell's biography, the scenario remains vague: something about childhood, dishonesty, and loss. But the story is told in broken pieces, without clarifying the relation between all the characters ("you," "she," "he," and "the children"). It was not until the 1990s that Mitchell began to speak openly to the media about the daughter she placed for adoption in 1965.[27] This was the key to the obscure, sorrowful aspects of "Little Green" (a coded reference to the child's name, Kelly). The song text incorporates reflections about the child's birth month and incidental details about the difficult decision while remaining discreet about the situation as a whole. In this regard it resembles Taylor's song "Fire and Rain" more than it does the other songs on *Blue*. Vocally, Mitchell provides a measure of relief from the prevailing melodrama by interpreting this song with a delicate, hushed beauty, keeping tight control over her emotions. At the melodic peak of each verse (*the children who have made her; she's lost to you; you're sorry, but you're not ashamed*) she allows her voice to sharpen and break into a wail before reining it back in. Arriving at the final word of the song (*sorrow*), she hovers on the edge of vocal fry. Only these tiny signs of vulnerability betray the pain beneath the unruffled surface.

"Little Green" derives its power from holding sadness *in* and freezing it into icicles—that is, beautiful images and elegant designs. All the other songs on *Blue* extravagantly pour their feelings out. In her prevailing approach to vocal performance on this album, Mitchell favors natural speech cadences, vivid characterization, intense expressivity, volatile (rather than controlled) gestures, and raw (rather than beautiful or polished) timbres.[28] She willingly sacrifices other aesthetic qualities for the sake of increased honesty and expressive power. For instance, in "The Last Time I Saw Richard," she jams up the melody with an overflow of words, vaults gracelessly into her high register, and allows her voice to lose tone at the end of each verse, all in the interest of vivid storytelling and emotional immediacy. The gesture that continues to resonate after the album has ended is her unexpected surge to a high belting undulation on "gorgeous wings": a last-ditch outpouring of hope in the face of depression. Joni once described her state of mind during the making of *Blue*: "At that period of my life, I had no personal defenses. I felt like a cellophane wrapper on a pack of cigarettes. I felt like I had absolutely no secrets from the world and I couldn't pretend in my life to be strong. Or to be happy. But the advantage of it in the music was that there were no defenses there either."[29] Singer-songwriters had already begun to lower their personal defenses in the service of artistic expression. In *Blue*, Mitchell took this approach to an extreme, tearing down her own protective mechanisms as well as any barriers separating listeners from her beating heart. It is this unprecedented openness that elicits such passionate attachments from her fans.

In a classic essay, cultural critic Richard Dyer shows how musical entertainment can embody a utopian sensibility: "Entertainment offers the image of 'something better' to escape into, or something we want deeply that our day-to-day lives don't provide. Alternatives, hopes, wishes—these are the stuff of utopia, the sense that things could be better, that something other than what is can be imagined and maybe realized." Musical genres can bypass narrative form to render such ideas in directly emotional terms, conveying "what utopia would feel like rather than how it would be organized."[30] What would it feel like to be free of inhibitions, to touch another person's soul with no dishonesty and no pretenses? Two of the categories of utopian expression identified by Dyer—*intensity* and *transparency*—are essential qualities of confessional song. As he argues, such forms of expression provide temporary answers to the inadequacies of the society we long to escape from. Dreams of intensity: if our modern world corrals us into dreary routine and careful respectability, then we will be fascinated by the person who ignores these strictures, emotes with abandon, and drains the cup of life to the dregs. Dreams of transparency: if only there were a special place where we could be honest, true, and open with others, as a remedy for those areas of life where we know we are being manipulated and misled.[31] The extravagant outpouring of confessional song gives us something we want deeply, even if it means taking the bad with the good.

For a while, Mitchell accepted the term widely used to describe her hyper-transparent aesthetic. In 1979 she remarked, "That's why I became a confessional poet. I thought, 'You better know who you're applauding up here.' It was a compulsion to be honest with my audience."[32] But in later decades, she has reacted ever more strongly against the label of confessionalism.[33] What does she object to? First is the tendency to reduce the meaning of the music to its autobiographical inspiration. Given the intimate connection between life and art in this genre, there is a danger that fans and journalists will treat the songs as romans à clef, documentary evidence to be charted against what is known of Joni's biography and attributed to one love affair or another. (During this period, Joni ended a serious relationship with Graham Nash, had a fling with Cary Raditz in Greece, and began a romance with James Taylor. "A Case of You" has also been linked to an earlier beau, Leonard Cohen.) But to do this, as critic Jack Hamilton has observed, is to imprison *Blue* in the stories surrounding it: "Fashioning someone's love life into a decoder ring to sleuth around music sort of misses the point of art."[34] Mitchell's purpose in exposing herself is never merely to document or draw attention to her personal experience. To fetishize the celebrity life story, as David Shumway explains so eloquently, is to misunderstand confessional art: "What such artists reveal is not an external cause of the work but emotional states the artist has experienced. In making these emotions available to an audience, the circumstances that gave rise to them are necessarily transformed.... Even though the emotions are real and details are taken from life, the songs are necessarily works of art or artifice, that is, fictions."[35]

This brings me to a second possible objection to the confessional label: that in construing songs as confessional in nature, listeners may treat them as *nothing more than* a direct outpouring of emotion; in other words, they may fail to appreciate the artistry involved. This has been a recurring refrain in the discourse around *Blue* from the beginning: don't forget that this is the work of a highly skilled artist! Appearances of spontaneous inspiration are deceptive. In his review at the time of the album's release, Billy Walker remarks on the exceptional honesty of Mitchell's approach: "You feel that each composition is a piece of the artist herself and that each new segment is exactly true to life, nothing however personal or painful has been left out." But honesty is only one side of the coin. "Whatever your likes or dislikes her artistry is unquestionable and whatever she does, like a champion prize-fighter, a great race horse or a Dutch master, it will be done perfectly."[36]

Meghan Daum has reflected at length on this common misperception. "The conventional wisdom about Joni is that she wears her heart—or even her guts—on her sleeve. There may be truth to that, but she also siphons out her messy emotions and rearranges them into coherent ideas, making for a very finely tailored sleeve." Unfortunately, Daum continues, most people are unable to tell the difference between *putting yourself out there* and *letting it all hang out*.

> Letting it all hang out is indiscriminate and frequently gratuitous. It's the stuff of paint flung mindlessly at a canvas . . . . Letting it all hang out is an inherently needy gesture. It asks the audience to do the heavy lifting. It dares the audience to

"confront the material" without necessarily making that material worth anyone's while.

Putting yourself out there is another matter entirely. It's an inherently generous gesture, a gift from artist to listener . . . . The artist who puts herself out there is not foisting a confession on her audience as much as letting it in on a secret, which she then turns into a story . . . . The point is that she had something to say and is saying it as artfully as she possibly can.[37]

The miracle is not that Mitchell cuts so close to the bone, but that she is able to channel that harrowing knowledge into well-crafted musical gestures and arrange them into a "perfectly sequenced collection" of songs.[38]

In performance, Mitchell creates a powerful impression of immediacy, as if she were sharing something of herself directly with the listener, making us believe that self and stage persona are one and the same, "that in other words there is no persona."[39] But this is an illusion, the effect of the language she has chosen and the style of delivery she has perfected. Her truth-telling self is a skillfully performed role, a fictional construction designed to project seemingly artless revelation.[40] The craftsmanship on display in *Blue* will be the topic of chapter 4.

Finally, stereotypes about confessional song can limit one's identification with the music. Joni puts it this way: "The beauty as a listener is you have an option. Either you can see yourself and your humanity in the songs, which is what I'm trying to do for listeners. Or you can say, 'That's the way she is' and equate the songs with me. The richest way, the way to get the most out of it, is to see yourself in it. The ones that do, whether they call it autobiographical or not, are getting it."[41] Think of Malka Marom's reaction when she first heard "I Had a King." As she remembers the occasion, in that song Joni made specific emotions available which struck a chord with Marom's own life experience. Joni conveyed a complex human reality with which she was able to identify and which carried the force of a revelation. "Joni Mitchell's songs have mattered to so many people not because of the individuals they may or may not refer to but because they help them make sense of their own lives, to understand their emotions, or to experience deeply someone else's emotional world."[42]

All artistic labels have shortcomings, and there is a long history of artists unhappy with the designations thrust on them by someone else. But we needn't do away with the label of confessional songwriting so long as we replace the reductive, stereotypical view of that artistic practice (as a "celebration of self-involvement") with a view of how it works in multiple dimensions as a "ritual exchange."[43] Here is Joni again, speaking in 2003, describing the kind of personal exchange she envisioned as she was writing *Blue*:

> I was demanding of myself a deeper and greater honesty, more and more revelation in my work in order to give it back to the people where it goes into their lives, and nourishes them, and changes their direction, and makes lightbulbs go off in their head, and makes them *feel*. And it isn't vague. It strikes against the very nerves of their life, and in order to do that, you have to strike against the very nerves of your own.[44]

Her words express utopian longings for greater self-awareness, authenticity, creativity, intensity, and transparency, within oneself and with others.

FIGURE 3.1 Joni Mitchell with artist Salvador Maron in Ibiza, 1970. Photo by Karl Ferris ©.

CHAPTER 3
ZEITGEIST

IN *DAUGHTERS OF AQUARIUS*, her study of women's role in 1960s counterculture, Gretchen Lemke-Santangelo features the personal recollections of women who participated in "hippiedom," or the lifestyle experiments of the baby boom generation. Conducted in the twenty-first century, her interviews probe the memories of older women casting their thoughts back to when they were "young, spirited, romantic, relatively privileged, self-absorbed, and caught up in the seemingly unlimited possibilities of the time."[1] As their contemporary, Joni Mitchell was noting down her experiences as she lived them and as they supplied material for her musical invention. In portraying the choices open to her and articulating her own exhilaration and confusion as she found her way, she was giving voice to perceptions shared by other young people of her generation. Mitchell told Michelle Mercer that *"Blue* is partly a diary. It's me moving through the backdrop of our changing times. I was in Matala and we got beach tar on our feet and then I went to Ibiza and I went to a party down a red dirt road.... But it's also more than a diary. It's one chapter in the Great American Novel of my work."[2] As in a novel, the locally observed narrative detail opens onto a social horizon. My aim in this chapter is to look outward from the protagonist herself to the backdrop through which she moves, the frame of reference that defines her as a child of her time.

LOOKING FOR SOMETHING

Joni Mitchell's career began during the emergence and rapid expansion of the counterculture in North America, when young people en masse expressed their alienation from mainstream society by dropping out of socially validated roles and routines, turning on to higher forms of consciousness, and tuning in to alternative values and ways of interacting with the world.[3] Many were alerted to systemic social problems like imperialism, militarism, and racism but "chose not to confront these forces directly; rather, they focused primarily on personal and cultural matters—music, art, theater, dope, mysticism, communal living—exploring themselves and developing particular interests and alternative values," believing that personal transformation would bring about a more humane society.[4] As an itinerant performer on the coffeehouse circuit in the mid-1960s and a denizen of a prominent artist's colony in

Laurel Canyon (a rustic neighborhood of Los Angeles) in the final years of the decade, Joni was immersed in this culture. (Two snapshots of canyon life: "Driving around up in the canyons there were no sidewalks and no regimented lines like the way I was used to cities being laid out. And then . . . there was the ruralness of it, with trees in the yard and ducks floating around on my neighbors' pond. And the friendliness of it: no one locked their doors." "[Frank] Zappa lived two doors down from me. My kitchen table overlooked his backyard, which is a pond that sometimes would have white ducks . . . and a raft that would occasionally have naked girls who'd float on it. . . . And my next-door neighbors were junkies who eventually burned their house down. . . . But it was a magical place.")[5] The language she uses on *Blue* often betrays a hippie accent: calling her live-in lover her "old man" ("My Old Man"), hanging out with "freaks" and a Daddy who's "outta sight" ("Carey"), describing friends as "the folks I dig" and displaying a tribal hostility toward the police by calling them "pigs," even when she's glad to see them ("California").

Though Joni didn't depict this cultural phenomenon for its own sake (except once, in "Woodstock," from *Ladies of the Canyon*), her musical self-portraits inevitably capture peripheral views of the milieu. More importantly, they reflect the emotional and existential tenor of a sensitive person living through such cultural upheaval. Changes were happening fast, the counterculture was not a single unified band of dissenters, and many of its forms of social expression were haphazardly organized.[6] There's a moment from the concert film *Celebration at Big Sur* (1971) where Joni conveys the hopeful but ill-defined nature of the movement.

The film—itself rather haphazard—documents the Big Sur Folk Festival held in September 1969 on the grounds of the Esalen Institute on the California coast, one month after the pivotal Woodstock festival. Mitchell was a featured performer, unveiling her newly written song "Woodstock" and leading her friends Crosby, Stills, Nash and Young in a rendition of Dino Valenti's anthem "Get Together." At one point, seated on the ground during a break, she tells an interviewer, "I guess it means a political revolution, and for some people it's a spiritual revolution. I'd like to believe that maybe people are getting more together."[7] This sentiment echoes the lyrics of the Valenti song, which suggest a groundswell of communal harmony (*Smile on your brother*) and a critical decision to be made (*You hold the key to love and hate / In your trembling hand*), while wrapping these high-minded aspirations in mystery (*Though the bird is on the wing / And though we don't know why*).[8]

For many of these young people, the choice to move against the tide meant a leap into the unknown. When they left home, defied parents, and rejected sensible careers to embark on personal or collective missions of liberation, they were abandoning conventional life paths "for an as yet undefined alternative."[9] They were "improvising their own ideal of adulthood."[10] Some were drawn to existing scenes that promised love or enlightenment: a nonconformist district in the city, a commune on arable land, an overland trek to Goa or Kathmandu. Others forged more individual paths, sounding out mystical traditions, psychedelic experience, or alternative psychology for guideposts to personal transformation. When Joni begins *Blue* by admitting she is "looking for something, what can it be," and "looking for the key to set me free," she is giving voice to an existential feeling shared by many of her fellow travelers.

While backpacking around Europe in 1970, Joni paid a visit to the village of Matala on the island of Crete, a place which hadn't been on her original itinerary.

> I was ready for an adventure. Penelope was a girl I knew [from Ottawa], and she was going [to Greece], and I asked if I could tag along. We were both friends of Leonard [Cohen], so we wanted to see his island [Hydra]. I brought a flute and my dulcimer. In Hydra I climbed to the top of a mountain and played among the goats and sheep with my flute. In Athens we went to this place where the poets hung out. . . . But everywhere we went in Greece, people would say to us, "Sheepy, sheepy, Matala, Matala!" We didn't know what that meant. It meant, "Hippie, hippie, go to the caves of Matala! That's where your kind are!"[11]

What she discovered there was a group of mostly North American expatriates who had found a congenial place to drop out, taking up residence in a "merry beehive of cliff caves" in a rocky beach cove near the tiny village.[12] She stayed for five weeks, living rough, hiking in the countryside, enjoying the company, and joining in the nightly music circles. Her sojourn on Crete provided the setting for the song "Carey" and one of the episodes in "California," both written for the dulcimer.

As I have written elsewhere, "Carey" embodies

> the attraction of a lifestyle unencumbered by routine or the pressure to conform. The life on Crete . . . is easygoing and out of the way. Caves provide natural shelter. One is thrown together with assorted colorful companions at the local

watering hole. Impulse reigns. The music in "Carey" is full of irrepressible energy, expressed in the continuous bouncing dulcimer pedal and the tune that springs up from its lowest to its highest point in a single leap. In the chorus, Mitchell and her friend dress up like roadside royalty for their night out. The village community allows for a relaxation of social conventions as well as a pocket of alternative culture where one can freely play with the symbols of status that prevail on the mainland.[13]

The song paints a picture of carefree existence, living for the pleasure of the moment, in a place where a Dionysian spirit reigns ("we'll laugh and toast to nothing and smash our empty glasses down") without regard for noble causes or rules of decency. And yet Mitchell makes the song much more interesting by revealing that the charms of vagabond life are wearing thin: nights too hot to sleep, inadequate personal hygiene, a craving for material comforts. She is ready to move on from the land of the lotus-eaters.

Whatever fulfillment Joni was hoping to find among fellow seekers on Crete, she was ultimately disappointed.[14] Taking precedence over any tribal solidarity was her personal quest for self-actualization, which sometimes inspired her to "move fluidly across the boundaries of bohemia," and at other times sent her down a lonely road.[15] When counterculture icon Timothy Leary took time to explain what he meant by his advice to drop out, he described it as a labor of discovery and an ethical practice: "*Drop Out* suggested an active, selective, graceful process of detachment from involuntary or unconscious commitments. *Drop Out* meant self-reliance, a discovery of one's singularity, a commitment to mobility, choice, and change."[16]

Mitchell maintains her focus on self-discovery by hewing to a confessional persona. She expresses a commitment to choice and change in the episodic progress of *Blue*, as she chases the elusive goals of authentic selfhood and authentic relationships. Joni-as-protagonist embodies mobility in her openness to adventure ("Carey": *Maybe I'll go to Amsterdam / Maybe I'll go to Rome*) and experimentation ("Blue": *I don't think so / But I'm gonna take a look around it though*). Mobility underlies the metaphor of turbulence that surfaces in "Blue" (*You've got to keep thinking / You can make it through these waves*). Motifs of maps ("A Case of You") and guiding stars ("This Flight Tonight," "A Case of You") reflect a certain anxiety over the unknown destination. Yet despite the risks, a readiness to move and change remains essential to the search. In "A Case of You," when the speaker's lover claims to be steadfast and unchanging (*I am as constant as a northern star*), he comes in for heavy scorn.[17] In the unusual presence of the easily portable dulcimer (never used again after *Blue*), we hear an acoustic trace of a vagabond season.

DEFINING HERSELF

Young people in the 1960s who chose to rebel faced different sets of head winds depending on their gender. "To be a girl, even in the context of 1950s 'permissive' childrearing practices, was to be neat, clean, well-mannered, obedient, helpful, domestically inclined, timid, and sexually pure. In contrast, boys were expected, if not actually encouraged, to be adventurous, free-spirited, and rebellious."[18] The adventurous subject of *Blue* is thus doubly transgressive, in refusing to be a "cog in something turning" ("Woodstock") as well as claiming a personal freedom normally reserved for men. Cultural historians have emphasized the singularity of this moment when women demonstrated extraordinary confidence in defying the old order. Lemke-Santangelo points out, for instance, that women's "experimentation with alternate spiritual traditions certainly had some historical precedents, but their drug use and largely unsupervised travels were completely out of the ordinary. Never before had such large numbers of young, middle-class women taken their search for self-realization in such radical directions."[19] Thus, dropping out had a special meaning for young women. It was, above all, an opportunity to escape "nuclear family-focused, suburban domesticity," the sexual double standard, and the limits imposed on female creative expression and physical autonomy.[20] From this angle, mobility meant not being trapped in a wifely role ("frau-duties," in Joni's words), and being free to explore an expanded horizon of female ambition.[21]

So, in addition to preserving personal observations of the countercultural milieu, *Blue* captures the perspective of a "struggling-to-be-liberated woman." As Judy Kutulas observes, "Mitchell's, [Carly] Simon's, and [Carole] King's songs and biographies were part of a growing woman-centered culture influenced by mainstream feminism and new demographic realities. [Their] songs suggested how the modern woman might straddle the line between . . . independence and desire."[22] Mitchell contributed to this discourse of modern womanhood on three fronts: by showing a woman taking control over her own image; by composing "narratives of sexual freedom"; and by working out nonconventional, egalitarian arrangements between romantic partners.[23]

Gretchen Lemke-Santangelo illustrates how the actual experience of women in the counterculture has been obscured by "layers of popular misconceptions, myths, and stereotypes that emerged during the 1960s and still persist." These include stereotypes spread by mainstream media—the hapless victim, the brainless, promiscuous chick, and the drugged-out, negligent mother—by which hippie women were belittled and decried as symptoms of moral breakdown. At the same time, "the counterculture generated its own images through male-dominated publications, art, and music—images that were just as shallow and distorted as those produced by external observers," promoting figures of male fantasy, such as the innocent virgin, the aggressive vamp, the cosmic love goddess, and the nurturing earth mother. In sum, "the vast majority of hippie women experienced little control over their own image."[24]

In contrast, Joni Mitchell's songs portray a woman of flesh and blood immersed in hip culture and tasting life's joys and disappointments. Instead of a fantasy figure, she presents herself as a real person who gets her feet dirty ("Carey"), who makes mistakes (as in "River": *I've gone and lost the best baby / That I ever had*), who succumbs to insecurity ("River": *I'm so hard to handle*) and doubt (*I shouldn't have got on this flight tonight*).[25] No wide-eyed innocent, she is a thoughtful person who faces risks head-on and navigates difficult choices ("Little Green"), who can silence a lover with a cutting remark ("A Case of You") or argue spiritedly against a cynical worldview ("The Last Time I Saw Richard"). When she does trade realism for mythopoetic imagery, her aim is not to project a feminine mystique but to deepen the symbolism of her path to selfhood. Thus in "Blue," she depicts herself as a seasoned sailor, prepared to leave port if her lover is unable to resolve his own troubles. In "The Last Time I Saw Richard," she imagines herself as an embryonic creature awaiting metamorphosis. Such metaphors reinforce an underlying drama of self-determination.

As for sexual matters, girls suffered under an extra burden of repression: "Middle-class parents not only placed more restrictions on girls' physical mobility but also expected their daughters to do a better job of containing their emotions . . . and sexual urges."[26] Emerging from years of such restriction and imposed ignorance, "at least initially, many hippie women had difficulty identifying and asserting their sexual needs and preferences."[27] As scholars like Judy Kutulas and Marilyn Adler Papayanis have shown, popular music was one place where young fans could encounter female subjects articulating their own desires and mapping out new possibilities for the liberated woman. Already in her first album, *Song to a Seagull*, Joni Mitchell presents an array of female characters expressing themselves as sexual beings: waking up with one's lover in the city ("Michael from Mountains"), frolicking au naturel by the seaside ("The Dawntreader"), pursuing one's own dreams while leaving a trail of attractive male conquests ("Cactus Tree"). *Blue* continues this pattern, rejecting the role of sex object and exploring "a new subject position for young women."[28] Mitchell's protagonists assert themselves, asking "Do you want to take a chance on maybe finding some sweet romance with me baby / Well, come on" ("All

I Want"), or "Come on down to the Mermaid Café and I will buy you a bottle of wine" ("Carey"); and facing the consequences of an unexpected pregnancy without shame ("Little Green"). They find memorable ways of embracing sexual pleasure in passages like "He's my fireworks at the end of the day" ("My Old Man"), or "the [star] that you gave to me / That night down south between the trailers" ("This Flight Tonight"), or "Lord, he loved me so naughty / Made me weak in the knees" ("River").

Such narratives of sexual freedom occur within a climate of "dissolving moral codes governing 'appropriate' sexual conduct for women."[29] As the social norms of chaste courtship, patriarchal marriage, and the nuclear family lost their cultural weight and moral authority, "middle-class youths were left to puzzle out their romantic identities [and] sexual values."[30] Mitchell's songwriting illustrates this sense of feeling one's way through new terrain and devising new models of intimacy. She writes about no longer needing a marriage certificate to remain committed ("My Old Man"), the attractions of casual relationships and pleasures of the moment ("Carey"), and "the search for a love that will liberate rather than confine" ("All I Want").[31] In "A Case of You," she puts an affair under a microscope, pondering her ambivalent feelings (*so bitter and so sweet*), weighing the benefits and the risks (*be prepared to bleed*), and basing her decisions in matters of the heart on compatibility and intensity rather than social approval. Beyond *Blue*, Mitchell's work is rich with examples of women negotiating with men, untangling their psychological complexities as they search for dignity and respect in love. The speaker in "Woman of Heart and Mind" (*For the Roses*) lays her cards on the table (*I am a woman of heart and mind / With time on her hands / No child to raise / You come to me like a little boy / And I give you my scorn and my praise*). She adopts a cutting voice, pointing out her partner's personality flaws and pushing him to change his priorities (*I'm looking for affection and respect / A little passion / And you want stimulation—nothing more*). But despite her misgivings she expresses commitment, looking past the bullshit to the person beneath (*You know the times you impress me most / Are the times when you don't try*).

In this way, Mitchell and other female songwriters "rewrote the formulaic love story" in popular music.[32] They fashioned their own response to the changes in the world around them, and in so doing, inspired others. The mass circulation of their music "helped to legitimize the new choices available to young women."[33]

A DREAM SOME OF US HAD

Another way Mitchell speaks for her generation, some have claimed, is in relation to the utopian ideals of the 1960s—that "decade full of dreams," as she called it in "Cactus Tree" (*Song to a Seagull*). As noted at the outset of this book, the music critics of the *New York Times* summarized the viewpoint of *Blue* as follows: "A restless woman travels, falls in love and longs for what she left behind as she moves on; in the background 1960's ideals crumble."[34] This portrait credits Mitchell with sensing the imminent decline of widespread visions of social change.

Jessica Hopper, writing for the *Los Angeles Times* on the occasion of *Blue*'s fiftieth anniversary, goes into more detail in support of this interpretation. According to Hopper, *Blue*

> captured the zeitgeist with its poignant portrayal of disillusionment. "Reading the news and it sure looks bad / They won't give peace a chance / That was just a dream some of us had," Mitchell sings in the opening verse to "California." At the time she was writing these songs, the Edenic dream of the Woodstock generation was confronting grim realities: the reinstatement of the draft, the Kent State shootings, the revelations of the My Lai Massacre and COINTELPRO campaigns against Black activists, [and] the dawn of the Weathermen.... "The Last Time I Saw Richard" and title track reflect the ebbing hope of the peace-love dream and growing cynicism, not just for Mitchell personally but for her generation.[35]

Three of the grim realities Hopper mentions relate to the Vietnam War; the other two denote violent episodes in domestic politics. The draft selections beginning in 1969 were devised to increase the number of military personnel available for war service.

> Youth felt betrayed. Nixon had promised to "wind down" the war—then, suddenly, he expanded it into Cambodia. Protest erupted: hundreds of thousands of students at over seven hundred colleges demonstrated. A national strike unfolded on a wide range of campuses, from hotbeds of activism in Berkeley and Madison to religious schools, community colleges, and southern institutions where little protest activity had existed previously. At two universities, demonstrations turned deadly. At Kent State University in Ohio, the governor called out the National Guard after rioters firebombed a Reserve Officers'

Training Corps building. On May 4 [1970], troops opened fire on students, killing four . . . and wounding eleven others. Tragedy struck again the following week when state police killed two African Americans at Jackson State University in Mississippi.³⁶

My Lai was a war crime committed by United States Army personnel against unarmed civilians in 1968, which went unreported until the following year. COINTELPRO refers to an FBI program of illegal surveillance, harassment, and disruption of American political organizations, including the Black Panther Party, whose leaders were targeted for neutralization. The program was secret until exposed by activists in March 1971. Finally, the Weathermen were a far-left militant organization founded in 1969 on the campus of the University of Michigan as a faction of Students for a Democratic Society. They pursued a strategy of violence with the aim of overthrowing the US government. Three of their members were killed in 1970 as they were making bombs in a Greenwich Village townhouse, when one of the bombs detonated.

David Shumway maps out a similar life cycle of 1960s idealism, marking the year 1968 as a turning point.

> Up until 1968, youth culture was hopeful about progressive change and about individual opportunities, but the events of that year [e.g., the assassinations of Robert Kennedy and Martin Luther King] began to alter the dominant outlook. . . . The antiwar movement would continue, of course, and the student strikes of 1970, which shut down more than 450 campuses in the wake of the Kent State shootings and the US invasion of

Cambodia, might be seen as the largest manifestation of the student Left, but also its last gasp.[37]

Such plot summaries, in which the spirit of a generation falters under repeated blows, or the outlook of a population sours from hope to cynicism, make for an overly pat narrative. In their sweeping, retrospective view, they bear little resemblance to the perspective of an individual living through these events. Remember that "youth culture" was not an entity with a harmonized outlook. It consisted of assorted groups of young people who set out to fashion an alternative culture "in an often disorganized but highly creative and idealistic manner."[38] Some groups expressed their opposition to the establishment purely in terms of a cultural revolution, while some engaged in political struggle. Thus, any attempt to gauge the vigor of "1960s idealism" by a single metric is futile. Moreover, for many young dissidents of the time, encounters with tragedy and oppression only strengthened their convictions. In Damon Bach's account, the "decline" of the counterculture that occurred in the mid-1970s represented not a waning of hope for change, but a shifting of energies toward the political sphere.

> To be sure, cultural activists still agitated for dope legalization and built counterinstitutions. . . . But many others resolved to effect lasting transformations in their lives and worlds through demonstrations and protest. This impulse manifested itself in efforts to elect George McGovern in the 1972 presidential contest, oust Richard Nixon after the Watergate revelations, and protest against the continuing . . . war in Vietnam. Others championed the women's movement, gay liberation, and the

American Indian Movement. . . . By 1974 most activists and freaks had hung up their alternative lifestyles after America withdrew from Vietnam, the draft ended, the economy stagnated, and the mainstream began to co-opt their values and styles. However, the counterculture's influence was immense and long-lasting, leaving a different America in its wake.[39]

Bach's assessment of the legacy of the 1960s casts doubt on the well-rehearsed tale of the demise of the utopian dream of the Woodstock generation. We can aim for more nuance by putting ourselves in the shoes of a young idealist caught up in the social turmoil and asking how they would have perceived the rumblings of change. The three Joni Mitchell songs mentioned by Jessica Hopper each offer a different reflection on social trends unfolding in the background of her private drama. In "Blue," she employs a seafaring metaphor to evoke a turbulent environment that is making it difficult for people to stay afloat. This general trouble or malaise is all the more ominous for being unspecified: Is it a loss of meaning? emotional fragility? despair in the face of social ills? After expressing a desire to "make it through these waves," Mitchell lists aspects of the hip lifestyle—hedonism and drugs—as if they helped people to cope while also implying that they are part of the problem. The blunt, ugly words she selects (*Acid, booze, and ass / Needles, guns, and grass*) contribute to a dystopic picture, a topsy-turvy world where a descent into personal hell is the latest fashion. In this example, Mitchell bears witness to the anarchic effects of cultural rebellion and the uncertainties of setting out on an unknown path.

"Blue" ends side 1 of the album by sinking to the depths. "California" opens side 2 with a renewed sense of cheer and excitement as the poet turns her thoughts toward home. Mitchell juxtaposes the vivid, picaresque adventures of the solo traveler in the foreground with the indistinct backdrop of political events she reads about in the paper. The news about the war looks bad; it "gives you the blues," in the symbolic language of color that runs through the album. But musically, Mitchell is careful to sustain upbeat emotions and keep the depressing thoughts from taking over. In fact, the opening lines, quoted by Hopper as a sign of disillusionment, are incongruously breezy. Instead of making heavy weather of the situation, Joni chooses understatement, as if dusting her hands off and refusing to cry over spilt milk. Especially after the wallowing of "Blue," the unsentimental good humor of this verse is refreshing, even a little silly. The unassuming turn of phrase (*That was just a dream some of us had*) expresses empathy with a small band of idealists, admits they failed to make a difference, and resolves to pick up and move on. Later reference to "the war and the bloody changes" is more serious in tone and affirms the ethical commitment beneath the irony.

Mitchell closes *Blue* with "The Last Time I Saw Richard," in which Joni recalls a philosophical conversation with a friend over drinks. Richard blusters that all idealists eventually lose faith and turn cynical, "boring someone in some dark café"—just as he is doing in lecturing Joni on her romantic illusions. The two friends don't use the word "idealists," however, but speak of "romantics" and "dreamers." At first the dreaming seems to be about love (*roses and kisses and pretty men; love can be so sweet*), but in the final verse it expands to encompass some alternative to middle-class conformity, some undefined hope for personal transformation. Joni tries to maintain her belief in the raptures of love (they're not just "pretty lies") and to deny that bitterness is inevitable. But Richard's surrender to a conventional marriage and an alienated home life weighs heavily on the protagonist, as if the loss of a fellow seeker seals her own fate. Drinking alone, her denials become more and more insistent until she bursts into a desperate plea for liberation (*before I get my gorgeous wings and fly away*). This song portrays disillusionment as a psychological struggle within individuals while implying that the affliction is endemic (*All romantics meet the same fate*; *all good dreamers pass this way*). The album ends with the protagonist undecided, caught between despair and hope.

In each of these songs, Joni channels disillusionment. But she does so in a diaristic voice, looking through a granular rather than a telescopic lens. It's misleading to link these episodes, as Hopper does, to a teleological narrative of "ebbing hope" and "growing cynicism, not just for Mitchell personally but for her generation."[40] Joni captured the zeitgeist not because she and her fellow idealists were all giving up on their dreams, but because she gave voice to the doubts that always shadow the quest for utopia. The topic comes up in an interview from 1972, where the interviewer states:

> We talk about the time she spent traveling [across Europe in 1970] and how—although songs came out of it and so it was a productive experience—there was an innate disappointment. A sense . . . of disillusionment that what she had believed would

be magical somehow never turned out that way.... "You tailor make your dreams to 'it'll be this way' and when it isn't—like, if you have a preconceived idea of anything, then inevitably it can't live up to your hopes."[41]

Utopian impulses are nourished by "an immeasurable and perennial desire" for a better world.[42] Visions of a hypothetical future inspire people to act toward finite goals, such as protesting military policy, establishing a principled community, or going on a pilgrimage. When these programs fail to bring enlightenment or solve the problems of the day, it is up to dreamers to manage their disappointment; the more idealistic the vision, the greater the risk of falling short. But utopia "has an energy of its own, which outlives the blueprint."[43] *Blue* has little to say about the collective efforts to build a better society taking place offstage. It zeroes in on one person living through a time of great hope and managing her disappointment.

CHAPTER 4
ARTISTRY

I suspect this will be the most disliked of Miss Mitchell's recordings, despite the fact that it attempts more and makes greater demands on her talent than any of the others. The audience for art songs is far smaller than that for folk ballads, and Joni Mitchell is on the verge of having to make a decision between the two.

Don Heckman, review of *Blue*, *New York Times*, August 8, 1971

I was only a folk singer for about two years, and that was several years before I ever made a record. By that time, it wasn't really folk music anymore. It was some new American phenomenon. Later, they called it singer/songwriters. Or art songs, which I liked best.

Joni Mitchell, interview with Cameron Crowe, *Rolling Stone*, July 26, 1979

Joni Mitchell's Blue. Lloyd Whitesell, Oxford University Press. © Oxford University Press 2026.
DOI: 10.1093/9780197686867.003.0004

> Today, there are a number of supposedly "pop" performers who are in no reasonable way distinguishable from "artists"....Joni Mitchell, who will be at the Forest Hills Tennis Stadium Saturday night, is such an artist—as serious and experimental as they come.
>
> John Rockwell, "The New Artistry of Joni Mitchell," *New York Times*, August 19, 1979

Joni Mitchell's musical style was under high torsion in 1970: a new recklessness in melodic design, a new elasticity of poetic verses, a voice venturing into extreme volatility. Together, these qualities convey the romantic, disheveled, unguarded persona so beloved by fans. Yet she never relinquished the careful attention to structural integrity, which had been evident in her songwriting from the very outset. Her leaps and dives in *Blue* rely on a strong backbone. Her pivots and swerves are gauged for maximum effect. Take the poetry from "All I Want." In its insistent first-person voice, repetitive babble, and gush of simple desires, the poem feels like a naive, spontaneous outpouring. But this artlessness is a construct, an expressive persona that distracts us to some degree from the underlying authorial technique. Artful design is everywhere evident in the regular internal rhymes (*strong, along, belong; talk to you, shampoo you, renew you*), alliteration creating parallels across verses (*alive, alive; applause, applause*), recurring repetition in twos and threes, and the use of puns and changing word forms to link adjacent phrases (*the living / Alive; I want / Do you want; my mind see-saws / Do you see*). Furthermore, at special moments the poet breaks the flow with reversals of perspective (*I am ... looking for something, what can it be / Oh I hate you some*) and shades her buoyant patter with darker threads of damage and insecurity. Throughout the album, no matter how fragile the dramatic persona, Mitchell wields a confident poetic technique to enhance psychological complexity, symbolic resonance, and emotional drama. Her lyrics exhibit "literary intent" as described by Mike Mattison and Ernest Suarez: "linguistically rich compositions that operate on many levels simultaneously, incorporating image, metaphor, narrative, linguistic nuance, and play in ways that often deliberately correlate to broader cultural conversations. . . .Lyrics that prick our curiosity and invite repeated visits and renewed scrutiny."[1]

In this chapter, the emphasis will shift from content to technique: not "what is she saying?" but "how does she do that?" I will adjust the focus from personal meanings to artistic presence: the sonic and poetic qualities that set Mitchell's songs apart for their beauty, intricacy, and sophistication. The emotional impact of the music will not be forgotten, but it will recede in importance as we attend to elements of design. My goal is to heighten awareness of Mitchell's compositional prowess and ingenuity, the dimension of her songs that allows listeners like Zadie Smith to forget their content and get swept up in their exquisite form. Appreciation of *Blue* involves a double exposure of the flawed and the sublime: its outpourings of human fallibility are couched in musical artifacts that outshine the work of many of her peers. In the following discussion, I will explore the aesthetic mastery on display in selected parameters of Joni's craft, to illustrate how "her seemingly unguarded revelations [are] so finely constructed."[2]

POETIC TECHNIQUE

In some of the songs on *Blue*, Mitchell purposely creates kinks in the flow of poetic ideas. By jumping from one type of expression to another, she suggests a disordered barrage of thoughts. "This Flight Tonight" is a prime example. Objective dialogue sets the scene: a pilot announcing that the airplane is about to land. A passenger tells us what she sees out the window. The flash of a falling star leads her to reflect on other stars, astronomical and metaphorical. In the chorus, she starts to make a wish (*Oh starbright, starbright*—alluding to the nursery rhyme), but swerves to address the lover who dominates her thoughts and whom she now regrets leaving. The second verse shares thoughts about this troubled relationship, interjects a note of general pessimism (*Sometimes I think love is just mythical*), returns to the view from the window, and ends by expressing an internal struggle (*Blackness, blackness dragging me down / Come on light the candle in this poor heart of mine*). The poem is a mosaic of disparate utterances—reportage, memory, handwringing, imaginary dialogue—indicating a distracted mind. Its surface discontinuities are held together by a simple meter and rhyme scheme, a focal source of anxiety, and the conceit of plane travel, which Mitchell exploits both for novelistic detail and the metaphorical situation of being up in the air, unable to change course.

Before this album, Mitchell's poetry was predictable in establishing a metric rhythm and a strong patterning of line lengths. The songs on *Blue* display more flexibility in this regard. The elastic treatment of poetic meter and line reaches its peak in "The Last Time I Saw Richard," a song notorious for its verbosity. Karen O'Brien contends that it "breaks all of the rules of lyric-writing; there's too much to say and too little time to say it but it works remarkably, becomes more like a spoken-word prose poem than a song."[3] Daniel Sonenberg remarks that the song's constantly varying line lengths defeat any sense of metric regularity, while Joni's vocal delivery evokes natural speech rhythms rather than the euphonious patterns of lyrical song.[4] If we count syllables in the first three poetic lines of each verse, we see that verse 1 has lines of fourteen, fourteen, and fifteen syllables; verse 2 ten, thirteen, and twenty-eight (!); and verse 3 eleven, sixteen, and twenty-one. (Identifying line ends by rhyme, the lines of verse 1 end on *'68, someday,* and *café*; verse 2 on *Wurlitzer, whirr,* and *close*; and verse 3 on *skater, percolator,* and *bright*.) Not only is there no consistency within or across verses, but certain lines far exceed the bounds of metric decorum. This extreme elasticity affects the rhyme scheme, which changes from verse to verse. Some verses contain internal rhymes (*Richard, you haven't really **changed**, I **said** / it's just that now you're romanticizing some **pain** that's in your **head***), while others do not. The third line is rhymed in verse 1 but unrhymed in verses 2 and 3. And the final verse stands out by ending with a hyperbolic outpouring of the same rhyme (*way, day, cafés, cafés, away, phase, café, days*).

Mitchell displays a masterly control of poetic imagery.[5] A song like "Carey" features vivid sensory snapshots of a specific lived moment (*My fingernails are filthy I got beach tar on my feet*). In contrast, the images in "My Old Man" are archetypal, collapsing stretches of time into a concentrated essence (*He's a singer in the park / He's a walker in the rain*). The song "Blue" explores a kind of modulatory free association. It begins with a simple comparison (*Songs are like tattoos*), but instead of explaining this unusual simile, the poet follows a tangent from tattoos to the idea of seafaring. The phrase "crown and anchor" evokes nautical body art; it's also the name of a dice game traditionally played by sailors in the Royal Navy. By turning the phrase into an appeal (*Crown and anchor me*), the speaker is challenging Blue to commit to their relationship or release her from it. In just four lines, the poet combines music, tattoos, seafaring, gambling, and romance into a composite set of metaphorical associations, too much to retain all at once. The interaction between symbolic domains is open-ended and multidirectional. If the referent of all these symbols is the first-person speaker and her intense emotions, she is casting herself in a redoubling series of imaginary roles: I'm a singer; I'm an illustrated body; I'm a sailor; I'm a queen; I'm a prize; I'm a ship. Associations beat at us in a turbulent flow. In the next four lines, we return to the starting point and learn why songs are like tattoos: they both use writing instruments; they're both indelible; they pierce the flesh; they fill a void; they get you hooked. We've moved on to a new figural composite of songs, tattoos, needles and pens, love and drugs. Instead of laying out a linear chain of thought, the beginning of "Blue" immerses us in a confluence of figuration.

These three aspects of poetic technique—heterogeneous utterance, elastic meter, and complex imagery—work together in "A Case of You." The poem consists of bittersweet reminiscences, scraps of dialogue, navel-gazing, and outpourings of love. Connections between the assembled passages are oblique, and the time frame is unstable. Each verse contains a memorable image, some of which are concrete (a map of Canada on a coaster in the light of a TV screen), some archetypal (the lonely painter living in her box of paints). When her lover invokes a romanticized archetypal image (*a northern star*), the speaker scoffs.[6] Yet in the chorus, she can't help resorting to a romantic image of her own (*You are in my blood like holy wine*). A contrast between elastic and regular meter helps to define the song's formal sections. Verses ramble in variable line lengths (syllable count in verse 1 = nineteen, twenty-two, sixteen, nineteen; in verse 2 = fifteen, seventeen, twenty-two, fifteen), while the chorus tightens up to ten- and eight-syllable lines. All through the verse, the dulcimer keeps up a constant dotted rhythm over which the vocal arabesques can freely unfurl. In the chorus, the voice homes in to align with this heartbeat rhythm for the crucial hook (*I could drink*).

FORMAL VARIETY

Mitchell generally works within the standard song forms in use in the North American popular idioms of her time: strophic, verse-chorus, and verse-bridge forms.[7] The songs on *Blue* are divided almost equally between these formal types. *Strophic* form refers to a succession of verses, each with the same musical pattern but different lyrics. "All I Want," "River," and "The Last Time I Saw Richard" employ strophic form. Joni embellishes "All I Want" and "Richard" (the opening and closing songs) with extended instrumental introductions and postludes. She rounds off the form of "River" with a partial return to the first verse, followed by a postlude. In *verse-chorus* form, the verses alternate with a chorus, a self-contained section with unchanging music and lyrics. "Little Green," "Carey," "This Flight Tonight," and "A Case of You" are in verse-chorus form. In "Carey," she varies the model slightly by altering the lyrics of the chorus, replacing the line "Oh you're a mean old Daddy . . ." with "We'll go to the Mermaid Café . . ." and including both lines in the final chorus. In *verse-bridge* form, verses alternate with a so-called bridge section, containing music that contrasts with the verse, while eventually preparing for the verse's return. Commonly, the bridge first enters after two statements of the verse. "My Old Man" and "California" use verse-bridge form. The former song ends with a statement of the verse, the latter with a fade-out on an extended version of the bridge (*Will you take me as I am?*).

Mitchell creates further variations on the standard formal types by including refrain elements. A *refrain* occurs when a portion of each verse always has the same lyrics. In contrast to a chorus, a refrain is not musically self-contained; it begins or ends incompletely. Refrains commonly appear at the end of verses, but they can be placed anywhere. "Little Green" incorporates a refrain element by beginning the last line of each verse with a statement of the song title. "My Old Man" includes an unusually long end refrain (*We don't need no piece of paper . . .*) that takes up half of the verse. Both "California" and "River" make use of split refrains, where refrain lines occur in nonadjacent positions. In the former song, the refrain (*California I'm coming home*) is interpolated at two points in the second half of the verse. In "River," refrain lines conclude the first two sections of the verse (*Oh I wish I had a river . . .*), as well as occupying most of the third section (*I wish I had a river so long . . .*), except for the final poetic line.

One song on *Blue* stands out for its sophisticated, unconventional form, not just in the context of this album but in Mitchell's work as a whole. "Blue" is through-composed, that is, it is based on continuous musical development rather than the repetition of coherent sections such as verses. The melody is made up of two recurring segments, uneven in length and prone to wandering. The first segment (call it **a**) always begins with the salient word "Blue" and usually follows the same chord progression (in the key of B). The second segment (**b**) features a repeated descending figure (*There's so many sinking*). The overall pattern of recurrence can be schematized as: **aa bb ba a**. But no recurrence is identical. The **a** segment is first stated with an extravagant flourish and a suspension of the meter, then repeated more succinctly and vigorously in the second phrase.[8] When **b** repeats in phrase 4, it switches from duple to triple meter and is quickly curtailed (*lots of laughs*), coming to a halt and struggling to regain composure. When it does recover forward momentum, the piano introduces a new harmonic color (the minor dominant). Phrase 5 is built from transposed repetitions of the **b** segment and leads directly into phrase 6, a climactic condensation and heightening of **a** (*Blue, I love you*). At this pivotal moment, the piano changes harmonic direction, moving through the minor dominant of B to cadence strongly on a different key (A). In fact, these four inserted measures constitute an almost exact quotation from the (A-major) introduction to "My Old Man," thus breaching the imaginary walls of this song and evoking the memory of a happier time. The final phrase returns to the original key and the **a** segment, while altering the harmony for a depressive sense of closure. Though an underlying symmetrical structure is discernible in "Blue," that symmetry is in constant danger of breakdown. The precarious structural situation adds to the expressive impact of the song.

MELODIC CONSTRUCTION

In her melodic designs, Joni Mitchell pays attention to pleasing contour, the expressive traversal of pitch space, and the placement of catchy musical ideas (hooks), as well as dynamic relations of balance, complementarity, tension, and release. The melody for "My Old Man" is relatively uncomplicated in its balanced phrase lengths (every vocal phrase is four bars long), joyous upward leaps, and syncopated, chromatic hook at the start of the refrain (*We don't need no piece of paper*). "River" sets up an alternating pattern in its contour: the first phrase is choppy, the second smooth, mimicking the imaginary glide of a skater. In addition, the verse expands in dimensions: after four four-bar phrases, the final two phrases stretch to six bars, just at the point where the singer is wishing for "a river so long." The expansion in phrase length coincides with the melodic highpoint (on the word *fly*). Such details show how Mitchell treats contour and phrase dimensions as expressive resources. By complementarity, I refer to relationships between open and closed phrases. (A phrase feels closed when it resolves harmonically on the tonic chord, and/or arrives by melodic motion at the tonic pitch.) In "River," the refrain structure divides the verse into two-phrase units: the first two of these units are open (*skate away on*), building anticipation for the strong conclusion of the third unit (*I made my baby cry*). Structural relations like these form the strong bones undergirding Mitchell's flexible realization of the melodic surface.

Popular songs of the time normally proceed in four-bar units. Since the listener generally expects balance between phrases, the introduction of imbalance can have an expressive effect, whether subtle or marked. (Bob Chorush noted this quality in a review of *Ladies of the Canyon*: "Joni's songs . . . seem to have an unevenness that makes them characteristic. Lines have little words and phrases toppling off them.")[9] Joni scatters irregularities throughout "A Case of You." She follows an initial four-bar phrase with a five-bar phrase. The slight adjustment in expectations is a rejection of the "constancy" professed by the ex-lover; it also gives us time to feel the sting of Joni's retort. The next two phrases are melodically parallel to the first two (we can diagram the four phrases of the verse as **abab**), so we expect the same phrase lengths. But this time, Joni breaks into phrase 4 with a tangential exclamation (*Oh Canada*) that adds an extra one-and-a-half bars.[10] The disruption of the basic meter draws special attention to her nostalgic thoughts. It turns out that this extraneous melodic snippet anticipates the hook occurring in the middle of the chorus (*a case of you*), which always creates a hiccup in the meter.[11] In another subtle avoidance of expectations, Mitchell delays the conclusion of the melody at the end of the chorus, as if savoring her intoxicated state. Ideally, the voice would align with the other parts by closing on the word "feet" as the harmony resolves to the tonic (on the downbeat). Instead, at that point the singer has only gotten as far as the word "my." By the time she concludes the line, the instruments have moved ahead into a new statement of their quasi-Baroque progression. Despite her claim to "still be on my feet," the misalignment between voice and accompaniment makes it sound like the singer has been swept *off* her feet by the forward movement of the instrumental cadences.

In its phrase construction, "All I Want" illustrates an extended interplay between balance and dynamism. The first section of the verse presents a complementary pair of phrases (one open, one closed), then restates that pair (**abab**). But the dimensions of this parallel structure are imbalanced. Every other phrase contains a metric disruption, coinciding with the syncopated hook (*Looking for something, what can it be*), where a beat (half a bar) seems to drop out of the meter. The **b** phrases are not as long as the **a** phrases, and the second **b** phrase is longer than the first (4 + 2.5 + 4 + 3.5). The next section (*I want to be strong*) begins with a chain of parallel open phrases (**cccc**), each merely two bars long, thus quickening the phrase rhythm. This sense of acceleration intensifies as the section continues. The final (closed) statement of **c** is cut short; the cadence on the tonic arrives a measure earlier than expected. Then the **d** phrase begins with even quicker melodic repetition at the half bar (*Do you want—do you want—do you want*). The phrase rhythm is propelled forward from four bars through two, then one, down to the breathless excitement of half-bar subdivisions. Mitchell combines this phrase acceleration with a gradual upward movement of the melodic contour, beginning in a low register for the **abab** section, expanding into a middle register for **cccc**, and climbing to a peak for the final line (**e**: *Do you want to take a chance on maybe finding some sweet romance*). Though the **de** section provides formal closure to the verse by balancing out the dimensions of the first half, it withholds harmonic closure. Both **d** and **e** phrases are harmonically unresolved, thus maintaining forward propulsion and building expectation for the return of **a** in the following verse.[12]

In contrast, "Little Green" emphasizes symmetry and elegance, despite the painful subject matter. The first, second, and fourth phrases of the verse begin with long mellow tones which proceed to unscroll in beautiful curves. Over the course of these four phrases, the voice climbs in a graceful arc to peak in phrase 3 (*the children who have made her*), then comes to rest on the tonic. At the close of verse 2, Joni releases the guitar accompaniment for a few beats, creating strong punctuation before the chorus, which has a lower contour and a distinct harmonic quality. At the same time, Joni binds verse and chorus together with a descending string of four notes from the opening phrase of the song (*moon in Cancer*).[13] This musical motive returns in the chorus as a cadential figure, stated twice at the midpoint (*crocuses to bring to school to-*) and three times at the end (*icicles and birthday clothes and sometimes there'll be*). The threefold statement of the motive creates a uniquely placed phrase extension in a song of balanced dimensions, amplifying the sense of closure as well as the admission of sorrow. Other salient features heard in the guitar are arranged to complement the overall design. The first thing we hear in the intro is a Bmaj7 chord—a very sweet sonority—animated by a gentle rhythmic swing. The second measure drops the swing for a more foursquare rhythmic profile and introduces a succinct cadential progression in which the bass line descends from the third degree of the scale to the tonic (3-2-1). The music from the intro continues as accompaniment under the vocal melody; thus the Bmaj7 chord accompanies the sustained vocal tones, and the 3-2-1 progression coincides with the descending motive in the voice. The third phrase breaks away from this pattern, creating uplift by moving to an E chord at the melodic peak. Phrase 4 returns to the initial pattern, with the voice now highlighting the major seventh (on the word "Green"). The chorus finds its own harmonic pathway by moving from E through a D chord (on the word "color")—a somber coloration since it implies B minor rather than the established major key. The double and triple statements of the main motive are supported by rhythmically augmented versions of the 3-2-1 cadence. In "Little Green," finely judged details of harmony, rhythm, voice-leading, contour, and phrasing work together within a shapely, orderly aesthetic.

HARMONIC SENSIBILITY

In a review of her concert at Carnegie Hall in 1972, Don Heckman asserts, "Joni Mitchell may be one of the most genuinely gifted composers North America has yet developed. That she chooses to express her art in small forms and personal sentiments in no way reduces either its impact or its importance." Among the qualities he finds exceptional are her unorthodox approach to the guitar, "brilliant harmonic sense, lyrical melodies and almost effortless poetry."[14]

Mitchell's distinctive sense of harmony is audible first of all in her chordal vocabulary, which includes a liberal use of nonstandard harmonies such as extended triads, suspended chords, and chords with added tones.[15] When writing for the keyboard, she frequently uses slash chords: triads in the right hand with nonchord tones in the bass. (Slash chords are so called from lead sheet notation, where they are written as upper triad then bass note separated by a slash: e.g., A/D, or "A over D.") Slash chords can be interpreted as extended triadic structures with the root in the bass (A/D would be Dmaj9), or in terms of independent strata, with the bass and upper layers projecting different harmonic paths and functions. The intro to "My Old Man" alternates pure triads with slash chords. The first chord in the right hand is a D triad aligning with the D in the bass; the second is a slash chord (A/D) with a complex, sharper relation to the bass. When the bass moves to E in bar two, the right hand plays D/E, an E triad, then a higher D/E—enriching the harmonic palette by moving in and out of slash chords while the bass remains stable.

"Blue" also exploits the expressive potential of slash chords. When the voice first enters, the right hand moves from Bm7 to A over a constant B in the bass. This chord progression is inherently ambiguous in its syntactical function. The latter A/B chord can be heard as a richly dissonant tonic sonority (Bm11). Alternatively, it can be heard as part of a neighboring chordal movement, since the right hand eventually returns to the Bm7; but neighboring motions don't usually stop dead in their tracks like this. Finally, the totality of the voice and piano can be heard as stratified into harmonic layers: the bass sustaining the tonic, the right hand moving from tonic to dominant, and the voice moving through the dominant to land on the tonic B in the second bar.[16] This economical gesture presents its harmonic material as multifaceted and conflicted. It packs an emotional punch, as Daniel Profeta demonstrates in his reaction video (see chapter 1).[17] With a similar complexity, the end of the first vocal phrase pauses to weigh the haunting effect of two parallel slash chords (D/G–E/A: *sail away*), with their multiple dissonances and open spacing.

Later in "Blue" (*lots of laughs*; *lullaby*), Mitchell introduces nontriadic chords in the right hand: an interval of a fifth surrounding a note a major second away from the bottom or top note. Some of these are suspended chords, that is, chords in which the middle note of a triad is replaced by a dissonant note, creating an unresolved quality. Others retain the middle note of the triad while adding a dissonant note above it. The chord sequence at "lots of laughs" can be notated in chord symbols as Em7(add4)–E7sus–Asus. The sequence at "lullaby" is Em7(add4)–E7sus–Em7(add4). A simple change of hand shape adds wrinkles to the harmony at these crucial moments. Such chords are commonly found in Joni's guitar writing as well. The first two chords in "This Flight Tonight" are A♭sus–A♭m7(add4).[18] The first sounds like an unresolved triad, the second like a minor chord with a dissonant addition. In this song, Joni uses the suspended chord to pivot between A♭ major and A♭ minor chords.

Pivoting between tonic major and tonic minor is an example of modal mixture, another important feature of Mitchell's harmonic sensibility. However, she usually avoids the minor mode (with its raised seventh degree and major dominant) in favor of the Aeolian and Dorian modes (minor-sounding, but with lowered seventh degree and minor dominant).[19] "This Flight Tonight" starts in A♭ Dorian, but by the end of the second phrase (*Las Vegas sands*) it cadences in a major key. The following phrase begins on A♭sus, allowing her to pivot back to Dorian for a restatement of the same progression. This tonal ambiguity reflects the ambivalent feelings of the speaker. "My Old Man" also mixes major and Dorian modes. Within the context of a sunny A major, Mitchell brings in a dark harmonic coloration by diverting for a moment to a tonic minor chord (*dancer in the dark*). In "Blue," the interplay between B Aeolian and B Dorian is more mercurial and pervasive. The Aeolian element (using G) is heard in G major and E minor chords, the Dorian (using G♯) in E major chords. These harmonic elements and the emotional polarities they suggest become closely entangled, as in the first vocal phrase. On the words "been to sea before," the chord progression is Gmaj7–D/E–E; on "sail away," Bm7–D/G–E/A.[20] (There are those parallel slash chords again, tangling G with G♯.) Some of the songs on *Blue* ("My Old Man," "Little Green") project a single dominant mode with occasional colorations from a different one, while other songs ("All I Want," "Blue," and "This Flight Tonight") are polymodal: no single mode prevails. While modal mixture does occur in the work of her fellow songwriters, Mitchell makes use of it to an unprecedented degree.[21]

Among the most unconventional treatments of harmony in Mitchell's work are songs that move between more than one tonal center.[22] She begins to explore this phenomenon in earnest on *For the Roses* (the album after

Blue), but *Blue* does include one polytonal song: "The Last Time I Saw Richard." The piano intro is in a different key (D Mixolydian) than the rest of the song. At the end of the intro (bar 17), Joni pushes the harmonies in a subdominant direction (G–C–F), rendering the key temporarily unstable. The next three chords (G–A–D) all sound like possible candidates for a tonal center, but the harmonies keep moving without confirming any one as tonic. When the voice enters at last, we have come to rest in the key of G. In the first four phrases of the verse, there is a prolonged emphasis on A minor (*all romantics*), which behaves like an upper neighbor chord, always returning to G. In the final two phrases of the verse, however, there is a push to the subdominant, recalling the destabilizing progression from the intro: G–C–F–G–A. At the conclusion of the vocal melody (*just pretty lies*), the harmony comes to rest on A for three bars, briefly tonicizing that pitch. At this moment, the relations between G and A are reversed, with G now the subordinate neighbor to a new tonic. At first, the A chord is suspended (will it be major or minor?), before it resolves to A major. This pivotal passage of tonal instability coincides with a point in the poem where the speaker (Richard) is intent on exposing his friend's illusions. Harmonically, we reach a positive resolution (A major), but it's not in the "right" key—maybe it's just a pretty lie. Mitchell develops a pattern of harmonic reinterpretation in this song: tonic D (intro) is recast as dominant to G (verse); tonic G (beginning of verse) becomes lower neighbor (end of verse); neighboring A minor (beginning of verse) becomes A major tonic (end of verse). This pattern of reinterpretation supports the drama of competing perspectives presented in the poem.

To extend the uncertainty even further, the song cadences in an entirely different key, B minor.

Alongside her forays into multiple tonalities, Mitchell has also written songs that explore a hyper-rootedness to a single pitch center by way of pedal points, that is, single notes maintaining a constant presence through changing harmonies. The use of insistent tonal anchors constitutes a distinct organizing principle. In guitar songs from other albums, the pedals are typically on the tonic, but in three of the dulcimer songs from *Blue*, Mitchell experiments with a dominant pedal. "All I Want," "Carey," and "A Case of You" are all in D♭, with the two upper strings tuned to a unison A♭. Joni leaves one of the A♭ strings (the dominant pitch) free to ring out in open tuning, while fingering the other two strings to create chord changes. But the low string of the dulcimer is tuned differently in each case: in "Carey" to D♭, a fifth below the other strings; in "A Case of You" to A♭, an octave below; in "All I Want" to G♭, a ninth below. The distinct tunings allow for different harmonic configurations. In "A Case of You," two outer voices separated by a tenth (an octave plus a third) proceed in a stately progression around the internal pedal, which is not perceived as a separate layer, just a note that's always there in every chord. In "Carey," the pedal creates its own rhythmic layer in a constant succession of eighth notes, while the other voices form intervals of fifths or sixths, sometimes enclosing the pedal note, sometimes launching high above it.[23] Both of these songs remain in a pure D♭ major, with no modal mixture.

Yet pedal points don't preclude an adventurous treatment of harmony, as we see in "All I Want." In the intro (which opens the album) the dulcimer's upper and lower strings move in parallel ninths, forming eccentric nontriadic sonorities, which emphasize C♭ and F♭ in the low voice and thus prevent the coalescence of a major key, while the A♭ pedal maintains a constant hyperactive pulse. Once the song proper begins, the upper string takes up the melody in D♭ major, while the lower string harmonizes at a (mostly major) tenth below. This parallel movement means that the low string voices C♭ (rather than C as in the tune) and F♭ (rather than F), resulting in an unstable modal surface. Some of the wayward tones pass by quickly, but at certain moments the harmonies come to rest on a C♭ chord (phrase 2: *Looking for something*; phrase 4: *Oh I love you*; final phrase: *take a chance*), establishing an expressive duality between this Mixolydian color and the major-mode context. At the coda (using C♭ as a pivot), the song returns to the eccentric gestures and nontriadic sonorities of the intro.[24] By stepping so far outside harmonic conventions, Joni conveys a "constant sense of surprise and discovery."[25]

VOCAL PROWESS

When English writer David Mitchell discovered Joni's album *Blue* as a youth, it "transformed [his] understanding of what songs could do and what singers could be." Her remarkable vocal abilities seemed to encompass the heights and depths of human drama. "Joni Mitchell's voice is made of contradictions: it warbles with vibrato but is astringent and harsh, too; it's acrobatic yet grounded; vulnerable yet indestructible; mannered and octave-straddling, yet also as natural as breathing."[26] The emotional journey Joni takes us through on this album is capacious enough to feature several distinct vocal personas. There's the off-the-cuff, unpretentious character of "California," favoring a fluty head voice with the occasional breathy quaver. There's the beautiful tone and burnished vibrato of "Little Green," a cool persona with hints of stifled passion. (Penny Valentine once described Mitchell in performance as a snow queen, her vocal line "pitched to hang like icicles on the night air.")[27] And there's the haggard voice of "Blue," now piercingly intense, now sagging with world-weariness.

Within each song, Mitchell displays a mastery of vocal nuance. Take "A Case of You," whose expression is relatively restrained for this album. The singer's clarity and poise convey a kind of truth-telling that is well-grounded, maintaining a sense of gravity even during difficult conversations. Joni handles the melody with a light touch while engraving its pitch contours with precision. Her vocal quality is generally fluty with little vibrato, so that when she wants to emphasize a word, subtle changes are quite effective. Thus in the second line, when relating her lover's assertion of steadfastness, the slight quaver on "constant" and the pitch bend on "northern" betray an undercurrent of disbelief on her part, which blossoms into an arch, strident tone by the fourth line (*I'll be in the bar*). After this brief outpouring, she returns to the prevailing delicacy of expression (*On the back of a cartoon coaster*). The pattern of unbuttoning, then reining in her voice recurs throughout the song, as in the first chorus, which rises with a piercing strength (*You are in my blood*), then pulls back to a quiet sweetness (*like holy wine*); or the second verse, which opens with a warm, vibrant exclamation (*Oh*) before pulling back again (*I am a lonely painter*). At the hook in the first chorus, the singer's delivery is pert and clipped (*I could drink*), only to melt into a continuous flow of vowels with extra tenderness in her enunciation (*you darling*). The same surrender to sonic pleasure closes out the chorus (*on my feet*), where Joni draws the final note into an exquisite silken thread, sustaining it well beyond its point of arrival. At each recurrence of the chorus, Joni invents spontaneous variations on the tune, with lavish expressive ornamentation on the word "darling." At the end of choruses 2 and 3, she opts for a different vocal quality, introducing pressure and a pronounced quaver (*my feet*), signaling passion and vulnerability within the relaxed aesthetic. Such commitment to ultra-fine detail, such a fresh perspective brought to every line, such intense vocal acting, all convince us that she is creating her melodies in the moment and singing them for the first time.

AESTHETIC DENSITY

As Don Heckman concluded in 1972, "what makes Joni Mitchell really special is the esthetic density of her music."[28] Her craftsmanship shows ingenuity in every dimension. Her richly textured language works on multiple levels. Her musical resources range from the pure and simple to the sophisticated and unorthodox. Her personal dramas stand out for their psychological substance: as she once said, she admires the Shakespearean model of "the dark soliloquy, with a lot of human meat in it."[29] In their beauty, finish, and sensuous impact, Joni Mitchell's songs reward repeated enjoyment and close attention; they have a captivating sonic presence. Technical analysis can only gesture toward that artistic dimension that remains beyond our understanding.

CHAPTER 5

EPILOGUE

ONLY A PHASE

For the entirety of 1971, Joni Mitchell retired from public performing. ("I came off the road," as she told a journalist the following year.)[1] After her solo evening at the Royal Festival Hall in London on November 21, 1970 (where she sang selected new material including "California," "A Case of You," "My Old Man," and "River"), she would not return to the stage for a major appearance until February 1972, when she launched an extended tour of North America.[2] Retirement in this case meant more than rest and recuperation: the artist was undergoing a full-blown personal crisis. When the recording sessions for *Blue* took place in February and March of 1971, "we had to close the doors and lock them while I recorded that [album], because I was in a state of mind that in this culture would be called a nervous breakdown. . . . I was defenseless as a result, stripped down to a position of absolutely no capability of the normal pretension that people have to survive."[3] "Nobody could come in. If anybody came in, I'd burst into tears."[4] Such extreme emotional fragility may have given her special insight as a musician, but it was clearly unsustainable.

In an attempt to regain a sense of well-being, Mitchell made a major life change, selling her home in Laurel Canyon and purchasing rustic land on the Sunshine Coast of British Columbia, where she could live close to the ocean. "I built a retreat up in the Canadian bush and swore I was never coming back."[5] When the songbook for *Blue* was published, it included photographs of the artist on her Canadian property, wearing a blue outfit with turquoise jewelry and lace-up boots: sitting on a tree stump playing the dulcimer, surrounded by rugged terrain, kneeling in the grass admiring a cluster of orange poppies.[6] Her new house was austere in design, "almost like a monastery. All stone and hardwood floors and hardwood benches."[7] Self-imposed solitude gave her the chance to commune with wild nature and read "every psychology book I could lay my hands on. Jung, Freud, theology, self-help, psychiatry."[8] Meanwhile she continued to write music and paint, away from the pressures of Los Angeles. She used this time to face inner conflicts and rebuild personal defenses, while exploring new directions in her approach to songwriting. Given her strong identification as an artist and the significance of her own lived experience for her art, the two objectives were deeply interconnected. One book about a classical composer, *Beethoven: His Spiritual Development*, written in the 1920s by J. W. N. Sullivan, made a profound impression.

> It was all about his struggles and self-doubts and his worries about how his work was being received and what it all meant on a deeper level and, of course, about his going deaf. At the time, that's just what I was thinking about too. How am I going to get back in the saddle? And what about the audience? Would you still love me if you knew what I was really like?[9]

Whatever her original motivations in running away from the music industry, she hadn't quite given up on a life as a singer-songwriter.

Prolonged seclusion and contemplation worked their magic, and in time Mitchell was able to sort things out.

> One day about a year after I started my retreat in Canada I went out swimming. I jumped off a rock into this dark emerald green water with yellow kelp in it and purple starfish at the bottom. It was very beautiful, and as I broke up to the surface of the water, which was black and reflective, I started laughing. Joy had just suddenly come over me, you know? And I remember that as a turning point. First feeling like a loony because I was out there laughing all by myself in this beautiful environment. And then, right on top of it, was the realization that whatever my social burdens were, my inner happiness was still intact.[10]

In this vivid scenic memory, deep symbolism is at work. Joni has discovered a space of well-being protected from external turmoil. Her emergence from dark water suggests a psychological breakthrough. In contrast to the transparent imagery she had used to describe her state of vulnerability

("I felt like a cellophane wrapper"), here the water's surface is reflective, guarding its secret depths. As opposed to the monochrome palette of *Blue*, here the visual field vibrates with black, green, yellow, and purple. The onset of self-consciousness ("feeling like a loony"), previously incapacitating, now fills her with a wild foolish energy.

Joni's statements about her music from around this time reflect a similar confidence and exuberance. When asked in 1973 whether she might lose some of her appeal by moving away from a vulnerable image, she replied categorically, "Well, I don't want to be vulnerable anymore." She insisted that vulnerability represented only one facet of what she drew on when creating music, and she wanted to expand the expressive possibilities, to show "a spectrum of a person's feelings, as opposed to locking into one facet."[11] Speaking in 1972 about the new album she was working on, she said, "This time I really want to do something different. Like, the music is already a growth, a progression from *Blue*, the approach is stronger and melodically it's stronger. . . . But I feel I want to go in all directions right now, like a mad thing right!"[12]

The songs she wrote while in retirement would appear on the album *For the Roses* (released November 1972). Of the twelve songs, half are written for piano, half for guitar. There is notable continuity with the preoccupations of *Blue*—traveling, searching, love troubles, and social ills. (Ellen Willis of the *New Yorker* described the album as "an elaboration of *Blue*—both technically and thematically.")[13] In "Let the Wind Carry Me," Joni evokes the call of the road (*Sometimes I get that feeling / And I want to settle . . . But it passes like the summer / I'm a wild seed again*). The speaker of "Barangrill" is restless and dissatisfied, chasing the pipe dream of ultimate fulfillment. Many songs divulge relationship woes, some in a first-person voice ("Lesson in Survival," "See You Sometime"), some in third person ("Blonde in the Bleachers"), one song mixing the two ("Electricity"). The album opens with "Banquet," which denounces the unequal distribution of wealth (*Some get nothing / Though there's plenty to spare*) while chronicling a diverse cast of dreamers who don't know how to find what they're looking for. In this song and others ("Lesson in Survival," "See You Sometime"), Mitchell employs the harsh wailing voice featured on *Blue*.

Yet at the same time, there are many ways in which *For the Roses* feels like a new chapter in the artist's journey. Her depiction of the search for fulfillment in "Barangrill" is relaxed rather than fraught. Though the speaker implies that she is troubled and anxious, she relates her predicament in a lighthearted way, enhancing the mundane setting with undertones of exotic adventure (*black diamond earrings, zombies,* and *Singapore slings*), and laughing at her own overexcited attempts to find Shangri-la in a cheap restaurant. In several songs, Mitchell replaces vulnerability with a strong, self-assured persona. The title song, for instance, voices a scathing critique of the music industry (while comparing herself to an exhausted racehorse, or a dog biting the hand that feeds her). The speaker in "Woman of Heart and Mind" asserts the dominant role in a romantic relationship, challenging her lover to rethink his priorities while cutting him down to size. The album closes with "Judgement of the Moon and Stars (Ludwig's Tune)," an homage to Beethoven and his defiance of social and musical convention (*You've got to shake your fists like lightning now / You've got to roar like forest fire*). As Ellen Willis points out, "recurrent images of electricity and fire [on this album] speak of a new kind of gathering energy, abstract and awesome—can it be anger?"[14]

In several of the songs already mentioned, Mitchell directs her gaze outward rather than inward: to flawed romantic partners, to the entertainment industry, to economic disparity, to renowned historical figures. (As she later said, in *Blue* "I peeled myself down to the bone, there was no place left to go. I had to start building up and healing myself and looking outward.")[15] Certain songs derive freshness and allure from their detached perspective. "Electricity," for example, mythicizes and abstracts its central human characters by representing them as components ("Minus" and "Plus") in malfunctioning circuitry. The song playfully spins out its metaphorical premise (*fuses and splices, masking tape, the technical manual, loose wires*) without explaining what actual relationship problems it might be referring to. Likewise, "Cold Blue Steel and Sweet Fire" creates a surreal picture of heroin addiction, peopled by fanciful figures more allegorical than human ("Cold Blue Steel," "Sweet Fire," and "Lady Release"). Both songs are highly artificial in their poetic conceits. Other songs with more personal poetic content still favor artifice over spontaneity in how they are constructed and performed. For instance, "Woman of Heart and Mind" sets up a pleasantly swinging groove in the guitar that never dawdles or alters. The vocal line stays within clearly defined tracks in each verse; any variations of rhythm or phrasing are relatively subdued.

The same aesthetic of clockwork precision in the guitar and self-containment in the voice is evident in "For the Roses." The turn toward artifice can also be seen in passages of verbal density where syntax is temporarily abandoned, allowing images to accumulate without showing how they logically connect. This occurs in "Cold Blue Steel" as part of a general unmooring from reality (*Underneath the jungle gym / Hollow-grey-fire-escape-thief*). It occurs in "For the Roses" when the fledgling poet is caught up in the race to stardom (*On your mark red ribbon runner / The caressing rev of motors / Finely tuned like fancy women / In thirties evening gowns*). When *For the Roses* was released, Michael Coates drew attention to the "increased use of metaphor and symbolism in her tunes. The change could be frustrating for listeners unable to fathom her sub-surface meanings, but for those who admire artistic word usage it should add another dimension to her excellent arrangements and distinctive vocals."[16]

Musically, Joni starts moving in bold new directions. She introduces jazz inflections such as the woodwind section on "Barangrill," the funky groove under "Cold Blue Steel," and Tom Scott's saxophone arabesques on "Cold Blue Steel" and "Let the Wind Carry Me." She makes a foray into orchestral arrangements on the latter song and "Judgement of the Moon and Stars," paired with ambitious formal expansions. Both songs pry open standard song form by taking off at midpoint into unpredictable instrumental journeys before circling back to the tune. At the time, several reviewers noted the strangeness of her latest venture, its "bizarre arrangements," and difficult concepts:[17]

> If you're going to like Joni Mitchell's new album *For the Roses* you're going to have to work at it some. As with all Joni Mitchell albums, the quality is there but on her first album for the Asylum label it's sometimes hidden quality. By that I mean even long time devoted Joni Mitchell fans like myself have to listen several times through before the meaning and value of some of the songs become apparent.[18]

Ellen Willis found the new album "even finer" than *Blue* in some ways. "Unfortunately, it is also less accessible. Joni's melodies and lyrics and rhythms are so rich and complicated and un-pop-song-like, her voice such a subtle instrument, her artistic pretension so overt that if the record were any less brilliant it would be a disaster."[19]

For the cover of the album, Joni had originally proposed a panoramic photograph of the ocean, with the artist herself, tastefully nude, standing on rugged rocks and gazing out to sea. Her managers insisted that this decision would be detrimental for sales (many retailers would refuse to display the product), and the photo was moved to the inner gatefold.[20] On a textual level, the image illustrates a line from the song "Lesson in Survival" (*I'm looking way out at the ocean / Love to see that green water in motion*). On a private level, it memorializes her period of retirement, since the photograph was taken near her home in B.C. It also strongly resonates with her personal healing narrative of jumping off a rock into emerald green water. With regard to her public image, it accomplishes several things at once. In its classical pose, flowing hair, and seaside setting, the nude portrait alludes to Botticelli's *Birth of Venus*, thus aligning with a high art aesthetic in an implicit rejection of commercial values.[21] In its remoteness from civilization, the image paints Joni as a free spirit, recalling the utopian ideals of hippiedom. But at the same time, it suggests a symbolic rebirth of the artist and an orientation toward the future, with her eyes on expansive new horizons.

In 2007, the Library of Congress added Mitchell's *For the Roses* to its National Recording Registry. The Librarian of Congress, with advice from the Library's National Recording Preservation Board, annually selects 25 recordings that are "culturally, historically, or aesthetically significant" to preserve for all time. By choosing this album over *Blue* or *Court and Spark*, both widely seen as highpoints in Mitchell's career, the Library expressed a dissenting opinion about the album most representative of her achievement. They provided the following rationale:

> In *For the Roses*, Joni Mitchell took the confessional lyrics of her critically-acclaimed *Blue* album and infused them with touches of jazz. The result is a mélange of folk, rock, jazz and country that retains the heartfelt tone of her earlier work, but presents it on a broader canvas. While Mitchell later delved more deeply into jazz, *For the Roses* remains the album in which all the elements of her creative palette are in perfect balance.[22]

The archivists sought to recognize Mitchell's music for its breadth and heterogeneity, and the hybrid nature of *For the Roses* gave a better sense of this than the focused purity of *Blue*. Looking back over her long musical journey, they froze this album in place, valuing it for the balance it supposedly strikes between multiple stylistic elements. This is not how I hear the album, however. To my ear, *For the Roses* is not balanced at all, but dynamic, joyfully overabundant, on the way from one place to another, exploding in all directions like a mad thing, looking for something without knowing what it could be.

Zadie Smith reminds us, "We want our artists to remain as they were when we first loved them. But our artists want to move."[23] There is the Joni Mitchell preserved at an incandescent moment in time, and the Joni disappearing around the bend; each to be treasured in their own way.[24]

NOTES

CHAPTER 1

1. Jon Pareles, Ann Powers, Ben Ratliff, and Neil Strauss, "Critics' Choices; Albums as Mileposts in a Musical Century," *New York Times*, January 3, 2000, https://www.nytimes.com/2000/01/03/arts/critics-choices-albums-as-mileposts-in-a-musical-century.html. The list is unranked.
2. "All-TIME 100 Albums," *Time*, November 2, 2006, https://entertainment.time.com/2006/11/02/the-all-time-100-albums/slide/all/. The unranked list was chosen by *Time*'s critics.
3. "The 500 Greatest Albums of All Time," *Rolling Stone*, December 31, 2023, https://www.rollingstone.com/music/music-lists/best-albums-of-all-time-1062063/jay-z-the-blueprint-3-1063183/. To compile the 2020 version of the ranked list, the publication "received and tabulated Top 50 Albums lists from more than 300 artists, producers, critics, and music-industry figures (from radio programmers to label heads)."
4. "The 150 Greatest Albums Made by Women," *NPR*, July 24, 2017, https://www.npr.org/2017/07/24/538307314/turning-the-tables-150-greatest-albums-made-by-women-page-15. This ranked list was conceived as "a correction of the historical record and hopefully the start of a new conversation. Compiled by nearly 50 women from across NPR and the public radio system and produced in partnership with Lincoln Center, it rethinks popular music to put women at the center."
5. "The 100 Best Albums of the 1970s," *Pitchfork*, June 23, 2004, https://pitchfork.com/features/lists-and-guides/5932-top-100-albums-of-the-1970s/. *Pitchfork* had established a reputation as contrarian-hipster and opposed to the mainstream; it also drew criticism for devaluing female and non-white artists. To its credit, the publication acknowledged the subjective nature of their ranking, describing it as a list of its "favorite" albums of the 1970s.

6. Jim Samson, "Canon (iii)," *Grove Music Online* (2001), https://www.oxfordmusiconline.com/grovemusic/view/10.1093/gmo/9781561592630.001.0001/omo-9781561592630-e-0000040598.
7. Samson, "Canon (iii)." "In a postmodern age, an age determined to expose the ideological and political character of all discourses, the authority of the canon as a measurement of quality in some absolute sense has proved increasingly difficult to sustain. It is threatened above all by a growing sense . . . that any notion of a single culture, of which the canon might be regarded as the finest expression, is no longer viable."
8. Rita Felski, *Hooked: Art and Attachment* (University of Chicago Press, 2020), 42–43.
9. Felski, *Hooked*, 53.
10. Ann Powers, "Her Kind of Blue: Joni Mitchell's Masterpiece at 50," *NPR*, June 20, 2021.
11. Colm Tóibín, "Three Weeks in the Summer," in *Heavy Rotation: Twenty Writers on the Albums That Changed Their Lives*, ed. Peter Terzian (Harper Perennial, 2009), 210.
12. Tóibín, "Three Weeks in the Summer," 204.
13. Tóibín, "Three Weeks in the Summer," 207.
14. Tóibín, "Three Weeks in the Summer," 205.
15. Tóibín, "Three Weeks in the Summer," 206.
16. Tóibín, "Three Weeks in the Summer," 209.
17. Tóibín, "Three Weeks in the Summer," 206.
18. Ruth Charnock, "'The Only Thing That's Never Going Away': Still Listening to *Blue*," in *Joni Mitchell: New Critical Readings*, ed. Charnock (Bloomsbury Academic, 2019), 205–6.
19. Charnock, "Only Thing That's Never Going Away," 204, 203.
20. Charnock, "Only Thing That's Never Going Away," 203.
21. Charnock, "Only Thing That's Never Going Away," 205.
22. Powers, "Her Kind of Blue."
23. Felski, *Hooked*, 18.
24. Daniel Profeta, "Joni Mitchell, thank you for this. REACTION to 'Blue,'" December 6, 2021, https://www.youtube.com/watch?v = vYfPpJfkgiU&t = 271s.
25. Hans Ulrich Gumbrecht, *Production of Presence: What Meaning Cannot Convey* (Stanford University Press, 2004), 107.
26. Felski, *Hooked*, 69.
27. Zadie Smith, "Some Notes on Attunement," *Feel Free: Essays* (Penguin Books, 2018), 100, 101.
28. Smith, "Some Notes on Attunement," 102.
29. Smith, "Some Notes on Attunement," 103.

30. Smith, "Some Notes on Attunement," 106.
31. Smith, "Some Notes on Attunement," 115–16.
32. Smith, "Some Notes on Attunement," 105.
33. Smith, "Some Notes on Attunement," 110, 105.
34. Smith, "Some Notes on Attunement," 116, 110.
35. Gumbrecht, *Production of Presence*, 99, 111, 113.
36. Gumbrecht, *Production of Presence*, 118, 99.
37. Gumbrecht, *Production of Presence*, 106.
38. Michelle Mercer, *Will You Take Me as I Am: Joni Mitchell's* Blue *Period* (Free Press, 2009), 2–3.
39. Smith, "Some Notes on Attunement," 115.

CHAPTER 2

1. Eliot Tiegel, "Joni Mitchell Clicks in 'Turned On' Act," *Billboard*, June 15, 1968.
2. Interview quoted in Christa Anne Bentley, "Forging the Singer-Songwriter at the Los Angeles Troubadour," in *The Cambridge Companion to the Singer-Songwriter*, ed. Katherine Williams and Justin A. Williams (Cambridge University Press, 2016), 84.
3. David R. Shumway, "The Emergence of the Singer-Songwriter," in Williams and Williams, ed., *Cambridge Companion to the Singer-Songwriter*, 11.
4. I draw on unpublished research by Rachel Avery on the formation of the singer-songwriter genre.
5. Nancy Murphy, *Times A-Changin': Flexible Meter as Self-Expression in Singer-Songwriter Music* (Oxford University Press, 2023), 16; Bentley, "Forging the Singer-Songwriter," 79.
6. Susan Braudy, "James Taylor, a New Troubadour," *New York Times Magazine*, February 21, 1971.
7. Daniel Levitin, "A Conversation with Joni Mitchell," *Grammy Magazine*, Spring 1996.
8. Al Rudis, "Joni's New Album a Personal Statement," *Cincinnati Enquirer*, August 15, 1971; Timothy Crouse, "Joni Mitchell, *Blue*" (review), *Rolling Stone*, August 5, 1971.
9. Alan Lewis, "How True Is *Blue*?" *Melody Maker*, July 10, 1971.
10. Billy Walker, "Beautifully Blue Joni Mitchell," *Sounds*, July 3, 1971.
11. Don Heckman, "Pop: Jim Morrison at the End, Joni at a Crossroads," *New York Times*, August 8, 1971.
12. Shumway, "Emergence of the Singer-Songwriter," 11.

13. For more on the distinction between lyric, narrative, and dramatic address in song texts, see Lloyd Whitesell, *The Music of Joni Mitchell* (Oxford University Press, 2008), 44–46.
14. Ariana Phillips-Hutton, "Private Words, Public Emotions: Performing Confession in Indie Music," *Popular Music* 37 (2018): 334.
15. Rudis, "Joni's New Album a Personal Statement."
16. Bill Flanagan, "Joni Mitchell Loses Her Cool," *Musician*, December 1985. Over the years, some of Mitchell's recollections have mutated and taken on baggage. Later versions of this story emphasize the idea that male singer-songwriters in particular were disturbed by the level of exposure. See the interview in Michelle Mercer, *Will You Take Me as I Am: Joni Mitchell's Blue Period* (Free Press, 2009), 25.
17. Meghan Daum, "The Joni Mitchell Problem," *The Unspeakable* (Farrar, Straus and Giroux, 2016), 155.
18. Interview (13:40), Susan Lacy, dir., *Woman of Heart and Mind: Joni Mitchell, A Life Story,* DVD (Eagle Vision, 2003).
19. Mitchell has acknowledged that "Laura exerted an influence on me. I looked to her and took some direction from her. On account of her I started playing piano again. Some of the things she did were very fresh. Hers was a hybrid of black pop singers . . . and Broadway musicals, and I like some things also from both those camps." Dave DiMartino, "The Unfiltered Joni Mitchell," *MOJO,* August 1998.
20. Shumway, "Emergence of the Singer-Songwriter," 15.
21. Shumway, "Emergence of the Singer-Songwriter," 16.
22. Todd Warnke, "Joni Mitchell, *Blue*" (review of remaster), *Soundstage!* May 1999.
23. Daniel Levitin, "Joni Mitchell," in *The Joni Mitchell Companion: Four Decades of Commentary,* ed. Stacey Luftig (Schirmer Books, 2000), 189. Entry written for *The Billboard Encyclopedia of Record Producers* (1999) but not included.
24. "Carey," "This Flight Tonight." In his review for *Rolling Stone,* Crouse contrasts the "mixture of realism and romance" and "occasionally excessive feyness" on the first two albums ("so reminiscent of Child ballads") with the more contemporary language of *Ladies of the Canyon* and *Blue*: "Like *Ladies, Blue* is loaded with specific references to the recent past, it is less picturesque and old-fashioned sounding than Joni's first two albums. It is also the most focused album."
25. "Carey," "California," "A Case of You."
26. Another early song, "Michael from Mountains," uses a second-person subject in the verse ("Michael wakes you up with sweets") and first person in the chorus. "Cactus Tree" casts its semi-autobiographical subject in the third

person ("she's so busy being free"). Both songs are from *Song to a Seagull*. See Whitesell, *Music of Joni Mitchell*, 52–53.
27. Karen O'Brien, *Shadows and Light: Joni Mitchell, The Definitive Biography* (Virgin Books, 2001), 255–57; Sheila Weller, *Girls Like Us: Carole King, Joni Mitchell, Carly Simon—and the Journey of a Generation* (Atria Books, 2008), 146.
28. Here I refer to analytical categories proposed in Whitesell, *Music of Joni Mitchell*, 60–63.
29. Cameron Crowe, "Joni Mitchell: The *Rolling Stone* Interview," *Rolling Stone*, July 26, 1979. In later versions, the metaphor becomes more grotesque: "I dreamed . . . I was a plastic bag with all my organs exposed, sobbing on an auditorium chair . . . . I wrote *Blue* in that condition." Malka Marom, *Joni Mitchell: In Her Own Words* (ECW Press, 2014), 57. The Marom book splices together interviews conducted almost forty years apart. The surrounding context suggests that this excerpt comes from the most recent interview, recorded in 2012.
30. Richard Dyer, "Entertainment and Utopia," *Only Entertainment*, 2nd ed. (Routledge, 2002), 20.
31. Dyer, "Entertainment and Utopia," 25–26.
32. Crowe, "Joni Mitchell: The *Rolling Stone* Interview."
33. See, for instance, Stephen Holden, "The Ambivalent Hall of Famer," *New York Times*, December 1, 1996; Mercer, *Will You Take Me as I Am*, 42–43.
34. Jack Hamilton, "Why Joni Mitchell's *Blue* Is the Greatest Relationship Album Ever," *Atlantic*, February 14, 2013.
35. David R. Shumway, *Rock Star: The Making of Musical Icons from Elvis to Springsteen* (Johns Hopkins University Press, 2014), 159.
36. Walker, "Beautifully Blue Joni Mitchell."
37. Daum, "Joni Mitchell Problem," 153–54.
38. Words of praise from fellow songwriter Carole King on the 50th anniversary of *Blue*. Dave Simpson, "Joni Mitchell's *Blue*: My Favourite Song—by James Taylor, Carole King, Graham Nash, David Crosby and More," *Guardian*, June 22, 2021.
39. Shumway, *Rock Star*, 160.
40. Phillips-Hutton analyzes the confessional mode as a form of "performative truth-telling." Phillips-Hutton, "Private Words, Public Emotions," 330.
41. Mercer, *Will You Take Me as I Am*, 7.
42. Shumway, *Rock Star*, 160.
43. I borrow Ann Powers's evocative phrasing. Ann Powers, *Traveling: On the Path of Joni Mitchell* (Dey St., 2024), 23.
44. Lacy, *Woman of Heart and Mind* (44:30).

CHAPTER 3

1. Gretchen Lemke-Santangelo, *Daughters of Aquarius: Women of the Sixties Counterculture* (University Press of Kansas, 2009), 6. Counterculture youth were predominantly white and from the middle class (35). "White, college-educated, middle-class boomers, who were economically privileged and able to experience more prolonged periods of personal exploration, were disproportionately affected by the so-called Age of Aquarius." Judy Kutulas, "'That's the Way I've Always Heard It Should Be': Baby Boomers, 1970s Singer-Songwriters, and Romantic Relationships," *Journal of American History* 97 (2010): 682.
2. Michelle Mercer, *Will You Take Me as I Am: Joni Mitchell's Blue Period* (Free Press, 2009), 22–23.
3. "Turn on, tune in, drop out" was a catchphrase popularized by counterculture guru Timothy Leary in print, audiovisual media, and public speeches, such as at the Human Be-In in San Francisco's Golden Gate Park in 1967.
4. Damon R. Bach, *The American Counterculture: A History of Hippies and Cultural Dissidents* (University Press of Kansas, 2020), xviii.
5. Barney Hoskyns, *Hotel California: Singer-Songwriters and Cocaine Cowboys in the LA Canyons, 1967–76* (Fourth Estate, 2005), 40; Cameron Crowe, "A Conversation with Joni Mitchell," liner notes, *Joni Mitchell Archives, vol. 2: The Reprise Years (1968–1971)*, Rhino, 2021.
6. In Damon Bach's account, the first phase of the counterculture emphasized cultural rather than political dissent: "there were appreciable differences between it, the antiwar movement, and student New Left." Its "diverse array of participants" included hippies, Diggers, Yippies, dropouts, Jesus Freaks, and other cultural rebels such as Andy Warhol and his clique. Bach, *The American Counterculture*, xi.
7. Baird Bryant and Johanna Demetrakas, dir., *Celebration at Big Sur* (20th Century Fox, 1971), 15:30.
8. Bryant and Demetrakas, *Celebration at Big Sur*, 30:00. Mitchell alters the words slightly from other recorded versions.
9. Lemke-Santangelo, *Daughters of Aquarius*, 4.
10. Theodore Roszak, *The Making of a Counter Culture: Reflections on the Technocratic Society and Its Youthful Opposition* (Doubleday, 1969), 33.
11. Crowe, "A Conversation with Joni Mitchell." "We found this floating poets' gathering place, and there was an apple crate of a guitar there that people played. I bought it off them for 50 bucks and sat in the Athens underground with transvestites and, you know, the underbelly running around—and it was like a romance." Jeffrey Pepper Rodgers, "My Secret Place: The Guitar Odyssey of Joni Mitchell," *Acoustic Guitar*, August 1996, 50.

12. Mercer, *Will You Take Me as I Am*, 15. Mercer quotes a 1968 cover story from *Life* magazine about the cave-dwelling community, whose author criticizes the young nomads for being "caught up in some sort of aimless journey toward an unknown destination" (16). For historic photographs of Matala and more details about Mitchell's experience, see Messynessy, "The Hippie Caves of Matala That Housed Joni Mitchell," *Messy Nessy: Cabinet of Curiosities*, April 21, 2015, www.messynessychic.com/2015/04/21/the-hippie-caves-of-matala-that-housed-joni-mitchell/.
13. Lloyd Whitesell, *The Music of Joni Mitchell* (Oxford University Press, 2008), 91.
14. Other reasons why she left the scene: it had become commercialized, people were getting crazy and reverting to primitive behavior, and the community was insulated from actual Greek culture. "Matala was full of kids from all over the world who were seeking the same kind of thing I was, but they couldn't get away from—I mean they may as well have been in an apartment in Berkeley as in a cave there because the lifestyle continued the same wherever they were." Penny Valentine, "Joni Mitchell Interview," *Sounds*, June 3, 1972. See also Larry LeBlanc, "Joni Takes a Break," *Rolling Stone*, March 4, 1971.
15. Lemke-Santangelo, *Daughters of Aquarius*, 47.
16. "Unhappily my explanations of this sequence of personal development were often misinterpreted to mean 'get stoned and abandon all constructive activity.'" Timothy Leary, *Flashbacks: A Personal and Cultural History of an Era: An Autobiography* (Jeremy P. Tarcher/Putnam, 1990), 253.
17. In her book on Mitchell's career, Ann Powers devotes an entire chapter to the theme of mobility and restlessness. Ann Powers, *Traveling: On the Path of Joni Mitchell* (Dey St., 2024), 65–111.
18. Lemke-Santangelo, *Daughters of Aquarius*, 11.
19. Lemke-Santangelo, *Daughters of Aquarius*, 5.
20. Lemke-Santangelo, *Daughters of Aquarius*, 22, 53–54.
21. Speaking in 1972 of her song "Cactus Tree" (*Song to a Seagull*), whose protagonist leaves behind a host of lovers in her quest to be free, Mitchell remarked, "I feel that's the song of *modern* woman. Yes, it has to do with my experiences, but I know a lot of girls like that, who find that the world is full of lovely men but they're driven by something else other than settling down to frau-duties" (Valentine, "Joni Mitchell Interview").
22. Kutulas, "That's the Way I've Always Heard It Should Be," 693–94.
23. Marilyn Adler Papayanis, "Feeling Free and Female Sexuality: The Aesthetics of Joni Mitchell," *Popular Music and Society* 33 (2010): 641.
24. Lemke-Santangelo, *Daughters of Aquarius*, 10, 23, 24, 25, 11. "Although men and women joined the counterculture in equal numbers and for equally

serious reasons, hippiedom's print record leaves the impression that women were peripheral to the movement and little more than decorative sex objects" (24).

25. Joni Mitchell: "When I began to write, women's songs were written by men, generally. And they were what men thought women should sing. You know, doormat songs. 'Someday My Prince Will Come.' They carried the old feminine values according to the master, right? My songs were of a different order, beginning to reveal feminine insecurities, doubts, recognition that the old order was falling apart. So I depicted my times." Chris Willman, "Joni Mitchell," *Entertainment Weekly Online,* March 2000.
26. Lemke-Santangelo, *Daughters of Aquarius,* 39–40. In this light, the confessional mode can be seen as a transgression of the demand for emotional containment.
27. Lemke-Santangelo, *Daughters of Aquarius,* 65.
28. Papayanis, "Feeling Free and Female Sexuality," 645.
29. Papayanis, "Feeling Free and Female Sexuality," 649.
30. Kutulas, "That's the Way I've Always Heard It Should Be," 683.
31. Papayanis, "Feeling Free and Female Sexuality," 646.
32. Kutulas, "That's the Way I've Always Heard It Should Be," 687.
33. Papayanis, "Feeling Free and Female Sexuality," 646.
34. Jon Pareles, Ann Powers, Ben Ratliff, and Neil Strauss, "Critics' Choices; Albums as Mileposts in a Musical Century," *New York Times,* January 3, 2000.
35. Jessica Hopper, "How Joni Mitchell Shattered Gender Barriers When Women Couldn't Even Have Their Own Credit Cards," *Los Angeles Times,* June 22, 2021.
36. Bach, *The American Counterculture,* 194.
37. David R. Shumway, "The Emergence of the Singer-Songwriter," in *The Cambridge Companion to the Singer-Songwriter,* ed. Katherine Williams and Justin A. Williams (Cambridge University Press, 2016), 11–12. See also Jules Witcover, *The Year the Dream Died: Revisiting 1968 in America* (Warner Books, 1997).
38. Lemke-Santangelo, *Daughters of Aquarius,* 8.
39. Bach, *The American Counterculture,* 250.
40. Hopper, "How Joni Mitchell Shattered Gender Barriers."
41. Valentine, "Joni Mitchell Interview."
42. Fátima Vieira, "The Concept of Utopia," in *The Cambridge Companion to Utopian Literature,* ed. Gregory Claeys (Cambridge University Press, 2010), 21. See also Amy Kintner, "Back to the Garden Again: Joni Mitchell's 'Woodstock' and Utopianism in Song," *Popular Music* 35 (2016): 1–22.
43. Vieira, "Concept of Utopia," 21.

CHAPTER 4

1. Mike Mattison and Ernest Suarez, *Poetic Song Verse: Blues-Based Popular Music and Poetry* (University Press of Mississippi, 2021), 4.
2. Jon Pareles, Ann Powers, Ben Ratliff, and Neil Strauss, "Critics' Choices; Albums as Mileposts in a Musical Century," *New York Times*, January 3, 2000, https://www.nytimes.com/2000/01/03/arts/critics-choices-albums-as-mileposts-in-a-musical-century.html.
3. Karen O'Brien, *Shadows and Light: Joni Mitchell, The Definitive Biography* (Virgin Books, 2001), 130.
4. Daniel Sonenberg, "'Who in the World She Might Be': A Contextual and Stylistic Approach to the Early Music of Joni Mitchell" (D.M.A. diss., City University of New York, 2003), 83–84.
5. For further discussion of poetic imagery, see Sarah Gates, "'Songs Are like Tattoos': Literary Artistry and Social Critique in Joni Mitchell's *Blue*," *Women's Studies* 45 (2016): 711–25.
6. The line about the northern star is a quotation from Shakespeare, *Julius Caesar*.
7. For extended discussions of formal principles in pop song, see Ken Stephenson, *What to Listen for in Rock: A Stylistic Analysis* (Yale University Press, 2002), 121–43; Drew Nobile, *Form as Harmony in Rock Music* (Oxford University Press, 2020).
8. In her book on the expressive use of flexible meter, Nancy Murphy describes the rhythmic stagnations in "Blue" in terms of a *loss of meter*, occurring in three places: the initial vocal entry, "lots of laughs," and "foggy lullaby." Nancy Murphy, *Times A-Changin': Flexible Meter as Self-Expression in Singer-Songwriter Music* (Oxford University Press, 2023), 112–13.
9. Bob Chorush, "Soft into the Garden," *Los Angeles Free Press*, April 17, 1970.
10. Thus the phrases of verse 1 have lengths of 4 + 5 + 4 + 6.5. Only verse 1 has the extra 1.5 bars.
11. Nancy Murphy describes the addition or removal of beats from an otherwise regular meter as *reinterpreted meter* (Murphy, *Times A-Changin'*, 28). She illustrates this technique in Mitchell's "A Case of You" and "All I Want," as well as in examples by Paul Simon and Cat Stevens.
12. The overall phrase structure is **abab ccccde**, with phrase lengths of 4 + 2.5 + 4 + 3.5 + 2 + 2 + 2 + 1 + 4 + 4.
13. This motive, a favorite of Mitchell's in her early style period, also appears in the piano introduction to "The Last Time I Saw Richard." See Lloyd Whitesell, *The Music of Joni Mitchell* (Oxford University Press, 2008), 181.
14. Don Heckman, "Concert Is Given by Joni Mitchell," *New York Times*, February 25, 1972. For more on Mitchell's approach to the guitar, see Jeffrey

Pepper Rodgers, "My Secret Place: The Guitar Odyssey of Joni Mitchell," *Acoustic Guitar*, August 1996; Peter Kaminsky and Megan Lyons, "'Chords of Inquiry': Alternate Tunings, Harmony, and Text-Music Relations in Joni Mitchell's Early Songs," *Music Theory Spectrum*, forthcoming.

15. For a discussion that places these chord types in stylistic and historical context, see Stephenson, *What to Listen for in Rock*, 82–88.
16. Nicole Biamonte interprets the passage as harmonically stratified in "Wide Harmony: Joni Mitchell's Slash-Chord Piano Voicings," paper presented at the conference "Joni Mitchell's *Blue* at 50," University of Connecticut, April 9, 2021. She interprets A (the subtonic) as a form of dominant.
17. Daniel Profeta, "Joni Mitchell, thank you for this. REACTION to 'Blue,'" December 6, 2021, https://www.youtube.com/watch?v = vYfPpJfkgiU&t = 271s.
18. The guitar is in an open G tuning with a capo on the first fret.
19. For a detailed explanation of modes, see Whitesell, *Music of Joni Mitchell*, 119, 126.
20. For a detailed analysis of harmony in "Blue," see Whitesell, *Music of Joni Mitchell*, 135–38.
21. For example, the Beatles tune "Eleanor Rigby" mixes Dorian and Aeolian modes; the Gordon Lightfoot song "If You Could Read My Mind" mixes major and Mixolydian (Whitesell, *Music of Joni Mitchell*, 126–27).
22. Walter Everett identifies songs by the Beatles with multiple tonal centers (e.g., "Good Day Sunshine," "Lucy in the Sky with Diamonds") in *The Beatles as Musicians:* Revolver *through the* Anthology (Oxford University Press, 1999). Christopher Doll discusses the general phenomenon of "centric ambiguity" in *Hearing Harmony: Toward a Tonal Theory for the Rock Era* (University of Michigan Press, 2017), 215–61.
23. The version recorded on *Blue* is enhanced with guitar and drums, making it difficult to hear the dulcimer arrangement. A performance with solo dulcimer is included on *Joni Mitchell Archives, vol. 2: The Reprise Years (1968–1971)*, Rhino, 2021.
24. A solo dulcimer performance of "All I Want" appears on the concert album *Miles of Aisles*, Asylum AB 202, 1974.
25. Rodgers, "My Secret Place."
26. David Mitchell, "David Mitchell on *Blue* by Joni Mitchell: 'It's art, so it's ageless,'" *New Statesman*, December 17, 2017.
27. Penny Valentine, "Joni Mitchell Interview, Part 1," *Sounds*, June 3, 1972.
28. Heckman, "Concert Is Given by Joni Mitchell." In her article, "'Poet-Composers': Art and Legitimacy in the Singer-Songwriter Movement," in *The Routledge Companion to Popular Music Analysis: Expanding Approaches*, ed. Ciro Scotto, Kenneth M. Smith, and John Lowell Brackett (Routledge, 2019), 416–25,

Christa Anne Bentley explains how "a discourse espousing the ideals of high art has served as a legitimizing strategy for singer-songwriters" (423).
29. Barney Hoskyns, "Our Lady of Sorrows," *MOJO*, December 1994.

CHAPTER 5

1. Penny Valentine, "Joni Mitchell Interview, Part 2," *Sounds*, June 10, 1972.
2. A chronology of appearances is archived on the official website, https://jonimitchell.com.
3. Jeffrey Pepper Rodgers, *Rock Troubadours* (String Letter Publishing, 2000), 43. The recording studios at A&M Records were busy places; friends were accustomed to dropping in on sessions, and other artists were aware of who was working down the hall. See David Yaffe, *Reckless Daughter: A Portrait of Joni Mitchell* (Sarah Crichton Books/Farrar, Straus and Giroux, 2017), 129–30.
4. Yaffe, *Reckless Daughter*, 133.
5. Vic Garbarini, "Joni Mitchell Is a Nervy Broad," *Musician*, January 1983.
6. Joni Mitchell, *Blue* (Charles Hansen Music and Books, 1971).
7. Marci McDonald, "Joni Mitchell Emerges from Her Retreat," *Toronto Star*, February 9, 1974. For more about the house and property, see Yaffe, *Reckless Daughter*, 150–51.
8. Richard Ouzounian, "Joni Mitchell Opens Up to the Star after Years Away from the Spotlight," *Toronto Star*, June 11, 2013.
9. Ouzounian, "Joni Mitchell Opens Up."
10. Garbarini, "Joni Mitchell Is a Nervy Broad."
11. Malka Marom, *Joni Mitchell: In Her Own Words* (ECW Press, 2014), 44. This interview was conducted for CBC Radio in 1973, in connection with the release of *Court and Spark*. A transcription is archived at https://jonimitch ell.com.
12. Valentine, "Joni Mitchell Interview, Part 2."
13. Ellen Willis, "Joni Mitchell: Still Travelling," *New Yorker*, March 3, 1973.
14. Willis, "Joni Mitchell: Still Travelling."
15. Michelle Mercer, *Will You Take Me as I Am: Joni Mitchell's Blue Period* (Free Press, 2009), 6.
16. Michael Coates, "Fifth Joni Mitchell Album Is Headed 'For the Roses': Lyrics Take New Dimension," *Van Nuys Valley News and Green Sheet*, December 8, 1972.
17. Don Shewey, "Joni, James Offer Strange Albums," *Rice Thresher* (Houston), December 7, 1972. "It is really the strangest record she has ever done. The songs are tremendously complex. . . .Luckily, the songs get better at each hearing."

18. Bud Newman, "Joni Changes Song Style," *Tallahassee Democrat,* December 3, 1972.
19. Willis, "Joni Mitchell: Still Travelling."
20. Photographer Joel Bernstein, quoted in Karen O'Brien, *Shadows and Light: Joni Mitchell, The Definitive Biography* (Virgin Books, 2001), 142–43.
21. Joni: "It was the most innocent of nudes, kind of like a Botticelli pose. . . . We were originally going to set that photograph in a circle and replace the daylight sky with the starry, starry night, so it would be like a Magritte." Cameron Crowe, "Joni Mitchell: The *Rolling Stone* Interview," *Rolling Stone,* July 26, 1979.
22. "*Thriller* in the Library of Congress: 2007 National Recording Registry Announced," May 22, 2008, https://www.loc.gov/item/prn-08-079/.
23. Zadie Smith, "Some Notes on Attunement," *Feel Free: Essays* (Penguin Books, 2018), 114.
24. The "complete songbook [is] an invaluable map for retracing the steps of one of the most amazing songwriting journeys of our time, while Joni Mitchell herself disappears around the next bend." Rodgers, *Rock Troubadours,* 55.

BIBLIOGRAPHY

"The 100 Best Albums of the 1970s." *Pitchfork*, June 23, 2004. https://pitchfork.com/features/lists-and-guides/5932-top-100-albums-of-the-1970s/.

"The 150 Greatest Albums Made by Women." *NPR*, July 24, 2017. https://www.npr.org/2017/07/24/538307314/turning-the-tables-150-greatest-albums-made-by-women-page-15.

"The 500 Greatest Albums of All Time." *Rolling Stone*, December 31, 2023. https://www.rollingstone.com/music/music-lists/best-albums-of-all-time-1062063/jay-z-the-blueprint-3-1063183/.

"All-TIME 100 Albums." *Time*, November 2, 2006. https://entertainment.time.com/2006/11/02/the-all-time-100-albums/slide/all/.

Bach, Damon R. *The American Counterculture: A History of Hippies and Cultural Dissidents*. University Press of Kansas, 2020.

Bentley, Christa Anne. "Forging the Singer-Songwriter at the Los Angeles Troubadour." In *The Cambridge Companion to the Singer-Songwriter*, ed. Katherine Williams and Justin A. Williams. Cambridge University Press, 2016.

Bentley, Christa Anne. "'Poet-Composers': Art and Legitimacy in the Singer-Songwriter Movement." In *The Routledge Companion to Popular Music Analysis: Expanding Approaches*, ed. Ciro Scotto, Kenneth M. Smith, and John Lowell Brackett. Routledge, 2019.

Biamonte, Nicole. "Wide Harmony: Joni Mitchell's Slash-Chord Piano Voicings." Conference paper, "Joni Mitchell's *Blue* at 50." University of Connecticut, April 9, 2021.

Braudy, Susan. "James Taylor, a New Troubadour." *New York Times Magazine*, February 21, 1971.

Bryant, Baird, and Johanna Demetrakas, dir. *Celebration at Big Sur*. 20th Century Fox, 1971.

Charnock, Ruth. "'The Only Thing That's Never Going Away': Still Listening to *Blue*." In *Joni Mitchell: New Critical Readings*, ed. Ruth Charnock. Bloomsbury Academic, 2019.

Chorush, Bob. "Soft into the Garden." *Los Angeles Free Press*, April 17, 1970.

Coates, Michael. "Fifth Joni Mitchell Album Is Headed 'For the Roses': Lyrics Take New Dimension." *Van Nuys Valley News and Green Sheet*, December 8, 1972.

Crouse, Timothy. "Joni Mitchell, *Blue*." Review. *Rolling Stone*, August 5, 1971.

Crowe, Cameron. "A Conversation with Joni Mitchell." Liner notes. *Joni Mitchell Archives, vol. 2: The Reprise Years (1968–1971)*. CD. Rhino, 2021.

Crowe, Cameron. "Joni Mitchell: The *Rolling Stone* Interview." *Rolling Stone*, July 26, 1979.

Daum, Meghan. "The Joni Mitchell Problem." *The Unspeakable*. Farrar, Straus and Giroux, 2016.

DiMartino, Dave. "The Unfiltered Joni Mitchell." *MOJO*, August 1998.

Doll, Christopher. *Hearing Harmony: Toward a Tonal Theory for the Rock Era*. University of Michigan Press, 2017.

Dyer, Richard. "Entertainment and Utopia." *Only Entertainment*, 2nd ed. Routledge, 2002.

Everett, Walter. *The Beatles as Musicians:* Revolver *through the* Anthology. Oxford University Press, 1999.

Felski, Rita. *Hooked: Art and Attachment*. University of Chicago Press, 2020.

Flanagan, Bill. "Joni Mitchell Loses Her Cool." *Musician*, December 1985.

Garbarini, Vic. "Joni Mitchell Is a Nervy Broad." *Musician*, January 1983.

Gates, Sarah. "'Songs Are Like Tattoos': Literary Artistry and Social Critique in Joni Mitchell's *Blue*." *Women's Studies* 45 (2016): 711–25.

Gumbrecht, Hans Ulrich. *Production of Presence: What Meaning Cannot Convey*. Stanford University Press, 2004.

Hamilton, Jack. "Why Joni Mitchell's *Blue* Is the Greatest Relationship Album Ever." *Atlantic*, February 14, 2013.

Heckman, Don. "Pop: Jim Morrison at the End, Joni at a Crossroads." *New York Times*, August 8, 1971.

Heckman, Don. "Concert Is Given by Joni Mitchell." *New York Times*, February 25, 1972.

Holden, Stephen. "The Ambivalent Hall of Famer." *New York Times*, December 1, 1996.

Hopper, Jessica. "How Joni Mitchell Shattered Gender Barriers When Women Couldn't Even Have Their Own Credit Cards." *Los Angeles Times*, June 22, 2021.

Hoskyns, Barney. "Our Lady of Sorrows." *MOJO*, December 1994.

Hoskyns, Barney. *Hotel California: Singer-Songwriters and Cocaine Cowboys in the LA Canyons, 1967–76*. Fourth Estate, 2005.

Kaminsky, Peter, and Megan Lyons. "'Chords of Inquiry': Alternate Tunings, Harmony, and Text-Music Relations in Joni Mitchell's Early Songs." *Music Theory Spectrum,* forthcoming.

Kintner, Amy. "Back to the Garden Again: Joni Mitchell's 'Woodstock' and Utopianism in Song." *Popular Music* 35 (2016): 1–22.

Kutulas, Judy. "'That's the Way I've Always Heard It Should Be': Baby Boomers, 1970s Singer-Songwriters, and Romantic Relationships." *Journal of American History* 97 (2010): 682–702.

Lacy, Susan, dir. *Woman of Heart and Mind: Joni Mitchell, A Life Story.* DVD. Eagle Vision, 2003.

Leary, Timothy. *Flashbacks: A Personal and Cultural History of an Era: An Autobiography.* Jeremy P. Tarcher/Putnam, 1990.

LeBlanc, Larry. "Joni Takes a Break." *Rolling Stone,* March 4, 1971.

Lemke-Santangelo, Gretchen. *Daughters of Aquarius: Women of the Sixties Counterculture.* University Press of Kansas, 2009.

Levitin, Daniel. "A Conversation with Joni Mitchell." *Grammy Magazine,* Spring 1996.

Levitin, Daniel. "Joni Mitchell." In *The Joni Mitchell Companion: Four Decades of Commentary,* ed. Stacey Luftig. Schirmer Books, 2000.

Lewis, Alan. "How True Is *Blue?*" *Melody Maker,* July 10, 1971.

McDonald, Marci. "Joni Mitchell Emerges from Her Retreat." *Toronto Star,* February 9, 1974.

Marom, Malka. *Joni Mitchell: In Her Own Words.* ECW Press, 2014.

Mattison, Mike, and Ernest Suarez. *Poetic Song Verse: Blues-Based Popular Music and Poetry.* University Press of Mississippi, 2021.

Mercer, Michelle. *Will You Take Me as I Am: Joni Mitchell's* Blue *Period.* Free Press, 2009.

Messynessy. "The Hippie Caves of Matala That Housed Joni Mitchell." *Messy Nessy: Cabinet of Curiosities,* April 21, 2015. www.messynessychic.com/2015/04/21/the-hippie-caves-of-matala-that-housed-joni-mitchell/.

Mitchell, David. "David Mitchell on *Blue* by Joni Mitchell: 'It's Art, So It's Ageless.'" *New Statesman,* December 17, 2017.

Mitchell, Joni. *Blue.* CD. Reprise, 1971.

Mitchell, Joni. *Blue.* Charles Hansen Music and Books, 1971.

Mitchell, Joni. *For the Roses.* CD. Asylum, 1972.

Mitchell, Joni. *Joni Mitchell Archives, vol. 2: The Reprise Years (1968–1971).* CD. Rhino, 2021.

Murphy, Nancy. *Times A-Changin': Flexible Meter as Self-Expression in Singer-Songwriter Music.* Oxford University Press, 2023.

Newman, Bud. "Joni Changes Song Style." *Tallahassee Democrat,* December 3, 1972.

Nobile, Drew. *Form as Harmony in Rock Music.* Oxford University Press, 2020.

O'Brien, Karen. *Shadows and Light: Joni Mitchell, The Definitive Biography*. Virgin Books, 2001.

Ouzounian, Richard. "Joni Mitchell Opens Up to the Star after Years Away from the Spotlight." *Toronto Star*, June 11, 2013.

Papayanis, Marilyn Adler. "Feeling Free and Female Sexuality: The Aesthetics of Joni Mitchell." *Popular Music and Society* 33 (2010): 641–56.

Pareles, Jon, Ann Powers, Ben Ratliff, and Neil Strauss. "Critics' Choices; Albums as Mileposts in a Musical Century." *New York Times*, January 3, 2000. https://www.nytimes.com/2000/01/03/arts/critics-choices-albums-as-mileposts-in-a-musical-century.html.

Phillips-Hutton, Ariana. "Private Words, Public Emotions: Performing Confession in Indie Music." *Popular Music* 37 (2018): 329–50.

Powers, Ann. "Her Kind of Blue: Joni Mitchell's Masterpiece at 50." *NPR*, June 20, 2021.

Powers, Ann. *Traveling: On the Path of Joni Mitchell*. Dey Street Books, 2024.

Profeta, Daniel. "Joni Mitchell, thank you for this. REACTION to 'Blue.'" December 6, 2021. https://www.youtube.com/watch?v=vYfPpJfkgiU&t=271s.

Rockwell, John. "The New Artistry of Joni Mitchell." *New York Times*, August 19, 1979.

Rodgers, Jeffrey Pepper. "My Secret Place: The Guitar Odyssey of Joni Mitchell." *Acoustic Guitar*, August 1996.

Rodgers, Jeffrey Pepper. *Rock Troubadours*. String Letter Publishing, 2000.

Roszak, Theodore. *The Making of a Counter Culture: Reflections on the Technocratic Society and Its Youthful Opposition*. Doubleday, 1969.

Rudis, Al. "Joni's New Album a Personal Statement." *Cincinnati Enquirer*, August 15, 1971.

Samson, Jim. "Canon (iii)." *Grove Music Online* (2001). https://www.oxfordmusiconline.com/grovemusic/view/10.1093/gmo/9781561592630.001.0001/omo-9781561592630-e-0000040598.

Shewey, Don. "Joni, James Offer Strange Albums." *Rice Thresher* (Houston), December 7, 1972.

Shumway, David R. "The Emergence of the Singer-Songwriter." In *The Cambridge Companion to the Singer-Songwriter*, ed. Katherine Williams and Justin A. Williams. Cambridge University Press, 2016.

Shumway, David R. *Rock Star: The Making of Musical Icons from Elvis to Springsteen*. Johns Hopkins University Press, 2014.

Simpson, Dave. "Joni Mitchell's *Blue*: My Favourite Song—by James Taylor, Carole King, Graham Nash, David Crosby and More." *Guardian*, June 22, 2021.

Smith, Zadie. "Some Notes on Attunement." *Feel Free: Essays*. Penguin Books, 2018.

Sonenberg, Daniel. "'Who in the World She Might Be': A Contextual and Stylistic Approach to the Early Music of Joni Mitchell." D.M.A. diss., City University of New York, 2003.

Stephenson, Ken. *What to Listen for in Rock: A Stylistic Analysis.* Yale University Press, 2002.

"*Thriller* in the Library of Congress: 2007 National Recording Registry Announced." May 22, 2008. https://www.loc.gov/item/prn-08-079/.

Tiegel, Eliot. "Joni Mitchell Clicks in 'Turned On' Act." *Billboard,* June 15, 1968.

Tóibín, Colm. "Three Weeks in the Summer." In *Heavy Rotation: Twenty Writers on the Albums That Changed Their Lives,* edited by Peter Terzian. Harper Perennial, 2009.

Valentine, Penny. "Joni Mitchell Interview, Parts 1 and 2." *Sounds,* June 3 and 10, 1972.

Vieira, Fátima. "The Concept of Utopia." In *The Cambridge Companion to Utopian Literature,* ed. Gregory Claeys. Cambridge University Press, 2010.

Walker, Billy. "Beautifully Blue Joni Mitchell." *Sounds,* July 3, 1971.

Warnke, Todd. "Joni Mitchell, *Blue.*" Review of Remaster. *Soundstage!* May 1999.

Weller, Sheila. *Girls Like Us: Carole King, Joni Mitchell, Carly Simon—And the Journey of a Generation.* Atria Books, 2008.

Whitesell, Lloyd. *The Music of Joni Mitchell.* Oxford University Press, 2008.

Willis, Ellen. "Joni Mitchell: Still Travelling." *New Yorker,* March 3, 1973.

Willman, Chris. "Joni Mitchell." *Entertainment Weekly Online,* March 2000.

Witcover, Jules. *The Year the Dream Died: Revisiting 1968 in America.* Warner Books, 1997.

Yaffe, David. *Reckless Daughter: A Portrait of Joni Mitchell.* Sarah Crichton Books/Farrar, Straus and Giroux, 2017.

ADDITIONAL SOURCES FOR READING AND LISTENING

THE OFFICIAL JONI MITCHELL website is beautifully curated and home to a wealth of information, including song transcriptions, a well-stocked library of articles from the press, and a chronology of appearances (https://jonimitchell.com/). Rare archival recordings have been published in the *Joni Mitchell Archives*, a multi-volume series handsomely produced by Rhino. The second volume (containing material related to *Blue*) appeared in 2021, the year of that album's fiftieth anniversary.

The principal biographies of the artist are Karen O'Brien, *Shadows and Light: Joni Mitchell, The Definitive Biography* (Virgin Books, 2001) and David Yaffe, *Reckless Daughter: A Portrait of Joni Mitchell* (Sarah Crichton Books/Farrar, Straus and Giroux, 2017). Sheila Weller explores Mitchell's life and achievement in the context of her female songwriting peers in *Girls Like Us: Carole King, Joni Mitchell, Carly Simon—and the Journey of a Generation* (Atria Books, 2008). A film documentary from 2003, *Woman of Heart and Mind: Joni Mitchell, A Life Story* (Eagle Vision, directed by Susan Lacy), incorporates valuable footage, especially from the early period, and features an authoritative interview with the artist. A set of career-spanning interviews led by Mitchell's friend Malka Marom is collected in *Joni Mitchell: In Her Own Words* (ECW Press, 2014).

Ann Powers's book *Traveling: On the Path of Joni Mitchell* (Dey St., 2024) delves into the many facets of Mitchell's image as a creator and cultural icon. Other studies evaluating her significance as a singer-songwriter include Marilyn Adler Papayanis, "Feeling Free and Female Sexuality: The Aesthetics of Joni Mitchell," *Popular Music and Society* 33 (2010), and a chapter in David R. Shumway's book *Rock Star: The Making of Musical Icons from Elvis to Springsteen* (Johns Hopkins University Press, 2014). Michelle Mercer has written the most extensive study of the circumstances surrounding *Blue*, in *Will You Take Me as I Am: Joni Mitchell's Blue Period* (Free Press, 2009). Ruth Charnock ponders the album's reception and cultural significance in "'The Only Thing That's Never Going Away': Still Listening to *Blue*," a chapter in her edited collection, *Joni Mitchell: New Critical Readings* (Bloomsbury Academic, 2019). Sarah Gates trains a literary-critical lens on the album in "'Songs Are like Tattoos': Literary Artistry and Social Critique in Joni Mitchell's *Blue*," *Women's Studies* 45 (2016).

My own book on *The Music of Joni Mitchell* (Oxford University Press, 2008) sets out a comprehensive framework for understanding Mitchell's artistic achievement in both music and lyrics. More focused analytical studies have recently begun to appear. Nancy Murphy's book *Times A-Changin': Flexible Meter as Self-Expression in Singer-Songwriter Music* (Oxford University Press, 2023) applies insights from rhythmic theory to several Mitchell songs.

Peter Kaminsky and Megan Lyons have launched a major interpretive project exploring the details of her highly individual guitar practice; an initial essay, "'Chords of Inquiry': Alternate Tunings, Harmony, and Text-Music Relations in Joni Mitchell's Early Songs," is forthcoming in *Music Theory Spectrum*.

INDEX

For the benefit of digital users, indexed terms that span two pages (e.g., 52–53) may, on occasion, appear on only one of those pages.

"4 + 20" (Stephen Stills), 23–24

"All I Want" (*Blue*), 6, 7, 24–26, 56–57, 61–62, 66–67, 70–71, 73–74
"Always, Joni" (Trousdale), 4
"America" (Paul Simon), 23–24
attachments, fans', 3–8, 28–29
authenticity, 16, 17–18, 19, 33
autobiography, 1, 19, 21–22, 24–25, 29–30, 35–36
awards and honors, 1–4, 87–88

"Banquet" (*For the Roses*), 82–83
"Barangrill" (*For the Roses*), 82–84, 85
Beethoven, Ludwig van, 80–81, 83–84
Big Sur Folk Festival, 37–38
"Blonde in the Bleachers" (*For the Roses*), 82–83
"Blue" (*Blue*), 6, 8–9, 50, 59–60, 63–64, 69–71, 74–75
"Blue Boy" (*Ladies of the Canyon*), 21
Browne, Jackson, 15–16
Buckley, Tim, 16

"Cactus Tree" (*Song to a Seagull*), 44–45, 46
"California" (*Blue*), 6, 51, 61–63, 74–75
canons, musical, 2–3
"Carey" (*Blue*), 6, 39–40, 59–60, 61–62, 73
"Case of You, A" (*Blue*), 29–30, 60–62, 65–66, 73, 75–76
Charnock, Ruth, 6–7
Cohen, Leonard, 16, 29–30, 39
"Cold Blue Steel and Sweet Fire" (*For the Roses*), 84–85
confessional mode, 1, 2–3, 18–33, 40–41, 87
"Conversation" (*Ladies of the Canyon*), 21–22
counterculture, 35–53, 86–87
Court and Spark, 87
Crosby, David, 15–16
Crosby, Stills, Nash and Young, 37–38

"Dawntreader, The" (*Song to a Seagull*), 44–45

disclosure, 1, 19, 20–21, 25–26, 28–29, 31–32
disillusionment, 1, 46–53
Donovan, 16
dulcimer, 39–41, 60–61, 73–74, 80–81

"Early Morning Rain" (Gordon Lightfoot), 23–24
"Electricity" (*For the Roses*), 82–83, 84–85
Eli and the Thirteenth Confession (Laura Nyro), 22–23
epiphany. *See* presence effects

"Fire and Rain" (James Taylor), 23, 27–28
For the Roses, 71–73, 82–88
"For the Roses" (*For the Roses*), 83–85
form, 57, 61–64, 85

"Get Together" (Dino Valenti), 37–38

harmony, 68–74
hippie culture. *See* counterculture

"I Had a King" (*Song to a Seagull*), 20–21, 32–33
idealism, 1, 46–53, 82–83, 86–87
immediacy, 10–11, 16–17, 20–21, 28–29, 32
intensity, 8, 10–12, 25–26, 29, 33
intimacy, 6, 16–18

John, Elton, 15–17
"Judgement of the Moon and Stars (Ludwig's Tune)" (*For the Roses*), 83–84, 85

King, Carole, 15–16, 42–43
Kristofferson, Kris, 19

Ladies of the Canyon, 65–66
"Last Time I Saw Richard, The" (*Blue*), 28–29, 51–52, 58–59, 61–62, 71–73
Leary, Timothy, 40–41
Lennon, John, 19
"Lesson in Survival" (*For the Roses*), 82–83, 86–87
"Let the Wind Carry Me" (*For the Roses*), 82–83, 85
Lightfoot, Gordon, 16
"Little Green" (*Blue*), 27–29, 61–63, 67–68, 70–71, 74–75
lyric voice, 19, 20–22, 24–25, 82–83

Marom, Malka, 20–21, 32–33
Matala, Crete, 35–36, 39–41
McKuen, Rod, 16
melody, 56–57, 64–68
Mercer, Michelle, 11–12, 35–36
"Michael from Mountains" (*Song to a Seagull*), 44–45
Mitchell, David, 74–75
"My Old Man" (*Blue*), 59–60, 61–65, 69, 70–71

Nash, Graham, 29–30
"New York Tendaberry" (Laura Nyro), 22–23
Nyro, Laura, 16, 22–23

poetic technique, 27–28, 56–57, 58–61, 84–85
presence effects, 8–9, 10–12, 57, 76–77
Profeta, Daniel, 8–9, 69–70

Raditz, Cary, 29–30
"Rainy Night House" (*Ladies of the Canyon*), 21–22
"River" (*Blue*), 5, 9–10, 61–63, 64–65

Sainte-Marie, Buffy, 16
"See You Sometime" (*For the Roses*), 82–83
self-actualization, 36–41, 43–44, 82–84
Simon, Carly, 42–43
singer-songwriter, 15–18, 20–21, 22–23, 55, 81
Smith, Zadie, 9–12, 57, 88

Taylor, James, 15–17, 29–30
"This Flight Tonight" (*Blue*), 58, 61–62, 70–71
Toíbin, Colm, 5–6
transparency, 28–30, 33, 81–82

utopia, 29, 33, 46, 47, 50, 52–53, 86–87

Vietnam War, 47–50
vocal delivery, 8–10, 17, 21–22, 25–26, 27–29, 74–76, 82–83
vulnerability, 4–5, 17–18, 19, 21–24, 28–29, 31–32, 56–57, 79–82

"Willy" (*Ladies of the Canyon*), 21–22
"Woman of Heart and Mind" (*For the Roses*), 45–46, 83–85
women's liberation, 6, 35–36, 41–46, 49–50
"Woodstock" (*Ladies of the Canyon*), 37–38, 41–42

Young, Neil, 16–17

Zappa, Frank, 36–37

www.ingramcontent.com/pod-product-compliance
Lightning Source LLC
LaVergne TN
LVHW041641060526
838200LV00040B/1667